CRAFT BEER BREWING
THE NEW WAVE OF BELGIAN BREWERS

CRAFT BEER BREWING

JEROEN BERT

THE NEW WAVE OF BELGIAN BREWERS

𝒧 | LANNOO

PROLOGUE

It was nearly freezing and the grass was covered with snow. Unpleasant circumstances to spend a whole day outside sitting still. But my two brewing buddies and I had a propane stove and a steaming kettle to warm ourselves. And the cold was perfect for brewing. Very few microorganisms — always ready to infect the wort and sour the beer — would hover through the air. A good day for our third attempt to brew an imperial stout.

Not that there was anything imperial about us that day, unless you have Napoleon's 1812 failed Russian campaign in mind. No, the three of us were just huge fans of stouts and we'd been told that high alcohol beers were easier to brew for newbie homebrewers. Hence, an imperial stout. We didn't know how to measure the amount of alcohol back then, but we had certainly been able to tell that our first attempt wasn't high in alcohol. It was light, flat and rather tasteless.

We kept our spirits high, keeping in mind that every brewer needs several brews to finalise a new recipe. However, ours wasn't a new recipe. We had found it on a homebrewers' forum — tested and tasted. And given the fact that our second attempt had turned out to be both higher in alcohol and a completely different kind of beer than the first batch, only one conclusion was possible: our problem wasn't a matter of fine-tuning a recipe. We were messing around in the garden, messing up the basics of brewing. And my terrace floor for that matter.

The brewday had started off well, until we noticed the smell of burning wood: the hot propane stove was scorching the terrace floor planks. Unlike the previous brew sessions, we had put the propane stove directly on the floor. Definitely not a good idea. Our wives and kids, though, had a wonderful day.

While trying to prevent things from getting worse, we had to turn off the stove and wait until we could touch it. It was enough to stop the brewing mid-process and screw up the beer. I have never been able to put my finger on the precise moment where things had gone wrong — the same lack of knowledge that keeps you from brewing well also keeps you from deducing where things go wrong. But when we first tasted the result of our third brew we knew right away it wasn't the imperial stout we had had in mind.

The result was technically beer and probably very representative of what beer would have looked and tasted like throughout history. Although I'm quite sure Napoleon's soldiers would have liked it somewhere in a snow-covered tent on the outskirts of Moscow, I quickly found out you don't make your friends happy and excited with a historically accurate beer.

Looking at the scorch stain on the terrace floor and with fingers nearly numb from the cold, I realised it was time to move inside, buy better and more accurate brewing equipment and, most of all, to learn more about the craft. I needed to get some advice from people who were not only brewers, but who had started as homebrewers themselves and had been more or less where I was now: at the very beginning of an interesting journey.

CONTENTS

8   **A JOURNEY IN RUBBER BOOTS**

1— How to brew in a bag

29   DOK BREWING COMPANY
17 — Kickstarting a craft beer revolution — **PALE ALE**

53   SIPHON BREWING
21 — The hoppiest — **IPA**

77   'T VERZET
25 — Sombre melancholy of the Russian soul — **STOUT**

103   BRASSERIE DU BORINAGE
29 — The Germans are back — **GOSE**

127   ATRIUM BRASSERIE ARTISANALE
33 — Honest, all-grain, no shortcuts — **CRAFT PILSNER**

147   L'ERMITAGE NANOBRASSERIE
37 — Thinking outside the box — **BEER-CIDER HYBRID**

173   ANTIDOOT WILDE FERMENTEN
41 — The hunt for the wild yeast — **WILD YEAST FERMENTATION**

197   CABARDOUCHE
45 — A farmhouse of the mind — **SAISON**

218   **33+33 CRAFT BREWERIES YOU NEED TO KNOW**

A JOURNEY IN RUBBER BOOTS

For the last ten to twenty years a new wind has been blowing through the richly flavoured Belgian brewing landscape. It is loosely inspired by the American craft beer revolution.

Despite an old brewing tradition in Belgium and the fact that most Belgian beer consumers are quite conservative in their preferences, brewing in Belgium is continually evolving. Some 'new kids on the block' in particular are moving forward, with remarkable beers, combining tradition and craft with innovation, guts, a healthy sense of humour and a lot of playfulness. Homebrewing has been growing in popularity for a long time, but in the last two decades lots of beer geeks have moved from brewing in their kitchens to founding their own professional microbreweries. Their business model is quite different from that of the established breweries. They choose to walk a different path, have a different approach, but do so with dedication, passion and in a very professional, skilled way.

This new wave of craft brewers values sustainable development, a spirit of collegiality and participation. Not just fancy words, but values put into practice. These brewers support each other's beers, on the assumption that beer lovers don't choose one beer over another, but like to taste them all. They are fuelled by the drive to develop new beers continuously, outside of their comfort zone and often in collaboration with fellow brewers.

In the past the Belgian beer culture was a strong influence on the American one; today the influence travels in the other direction. The new wave of Belgian beer follows a new wave of American craft beers, which echoes all over the world. And yet, the Belgian new wave is not just a pale copy. American influences are infused smoothly into the rich Belgian tradition, resulting in a whole range of new, fantastic beers — which at the end of the day is what matters.

In a way the growing number of craft brewers in Belgium is a journey back in time, to the era when Belgian cities and villages housed numerous smaller breweries. Around 1900 there were 3200 breweries in Belgium. Today, even with many new city breweries, micro- and nanobreweries, those numbers are beyond reach. The quality, variety and availability, however, have never been better.

CRAFT OR ARTISANAL?

For *Craft Beer Brewing: The New Wave of Belgian Brewers* I put on my rubber boots — one of a brewer's main 'weapons' — and went on a journey with this new wave of brewers to discover their craft and their well-crafted beers. I joined them on a brewday, a day of blending, or any other work they do either to produce their beers or to bring them to an audience, organising a beer festival for instance. As a homebrewer I used this experience to raise my homebrews to a higher level and develop new, easy to brew recipes that reflect the variety of craft beer styles. Along the way I discovered and practised a fairly new and accessible brew method — brew in a bag (BIAB) — that allows homebrewers to brew small, quality batches in their kitchens.
I hope to show you how delightful and adventurous craft beers can be and how dedicated and skilled these brewers are. The result, however, is not a book about every craft beer or craft brewery in Belgium. Instead, I spent a day at eight breweries, choosing to tell their story in depth and share their everyday brewing

practices as an example of what drives this new wave of Belgian brewers and what is happening on the craft beer scene.

The absence of more traditional brewers in this book does not imply they aren't brewing well-crafted beers. In a Belgian context it is important to make a distinction between the term 'craft' and 'artisanal', synonyms in English, but not in Dutch or French. Belgium has many artisanal breweries, making great beers, much appreciated all over the world. Technically this new wave of brewers fits into this category. But these young wolves also use the term 'craft brewer' to describe themselves and to point out that they're into brewing in the spirit of the American craft beer revolution: they want to push boundaries and sacrifice sacred cows in an artisanal way.

The selection of brewers and stories in this book was made with very distinctive criteria in mind. For one thing, because adventure and the drive to keep on creating new beers are crucial to this new wave, I wanted to visit brewers who bring new, challenging and very diverse beers to the market on a regular basis. And I wanted the selection to be geographically diverse too, giving a representative idea of what's going on throughout Belgium in terms of craft beer.

A COLOURFUL NETWORK

Very early in the process of writing this book, one characteristic of these brewers caught my attention: the eagerness to collaborate with other brewers — Belgian and non-Belgian — and the fact that these collaborations are not based on a commercial strategy. It made me think of times, long ago, when I was playing in a (totally unknown and short-lived) music band. We sure drank a lot of beer in dirty backstage dressing rooms. We shared the rehearsal space with other bands. We passed on cassettes (yes, cassettes!) with music of newly discovered and often obscure bands. We shared instruments and microphones, went to each other's gigs and were the first to start stage diving to set the rest of the thin crowd in motion. And we collaborated: backing vocals on a demo, additional rhythm instruments, plain noise in the background...

Looking back, I realise we had a 'network' and it served two goals: to make better music and to have fun. It's a similar type of network I saw in this new wave of craft brewers and I am following it throughout this book. As a matter of fact, once I made contact with one brewer the others — fellow brewers, kindred spirits — followed in a very organic way. This network, however, does not equate to uniformity. These brewers share certain characteristics, but also show a lot of variation in approach, favoured beer styles and even brewing philosophy.

'Craft beer' and 'craft brewing' aren't well-defined categories and the terms provoke some debate. In every chapter I ask a craft brewer what his or her definition of 'craft beer' and 'craft brewing' is. The answers turned out to reveal very clearly the ways in which these brewers are both kindred spirits and headstrong minds at the same time.

I am very thankful to them for putting up with me for one brewday and sharing with me their knowhow, passion and insights on beer and brewing. I thought I knew a thing or two about beer, but this journey has been a real eye-opener. I hope this book will be one for you, too.

How to brew in a bag

The first time I visited a brewery, many years ago, the brewer compared the brewing process, mashing in particular, to making a cup of tea. Brewing in a bag is exactly that: it is making grain tea. And all you need is a kettle, a brewbag and some sort of container to let your 'tea' ferment. There are other things that might be helpful, but basically this is all you need.

Because it's a very easy and cheap brewing method, with less clean-up and ideal for brewing smaller batches, you can brew in your kitchen without having to reorganise the place. That's why you will probably brew more frequently and become a better, more experienced homebrewer, trying your hand at a larger variety of beers. At least that's what I did, with the recipes in this book as a result.

Another reason why I chose to dig into brewing in a bag is because it's an easy small-batch all-grain brewing method, which allowed me, in contrast with extract brewing, to go through the whole process from start to finish. It made me feel like the outcome was really *my* beer.

There is a downside too, though. Unlike the nearly closed system most professional craft brewers use, you won't be able to control every aspect of brewing. Your beer will be in contact with oxygen, which may cause oxidation, so all you can do is try to minimise that. With a lot of hot malts in hot water in a tight space like your brewkettle, mash temperature is hard to measure exactly and will not always obey your will. But by starting at the right strike temperature you will be able to prevent temperature problems. And at the end of a brewday you might end up at some point with one litre short or more gravity than you had wished for (because more water has evaporated or has been absorbed by the grist than theoretically predicted). Well, there are ways to adjust this (some as simple as adding some more water to the wort). But you shouldn't care too much if that happens. To enjoy a glass of your homebrew you need to brew it in the first place. And should anything go wrong and your beer isn't perfect, it doesn't necessarily mean your beer is too bad to drink. If you follow the basic rules, you won't screw up your beer (though there may be room for improvement).

However, this could be different once you start experimenting with wild yeast and kettle souring. You will be, well, experimenting. With mixed results. But hey, isn't that the whole point of homebrewing? When you don't give up after a failed experiment and you try to do it better next time, you do what craft brewers do: you are perfecting your brewing skills, you're pushing the boundaries and you are trying to leave your mark on a popular beer style.

And for what it's worth, the recipes in this book have been tested and approved (not unanimously, tastes differ), but that doesn't mean another homebrewer or I can't make them better. A different hop or yeast, another malt added to the malt bill, aiming for a higher original gravity, more body or a lighter body... These recipes could be a starting point to develop new recipes. They will for me.

WHAT YOU NEED

THE BARE NECESSITIES
— A stainless steel kettle of 20 litres (or 30, though larger will be less handy) to serve as your mash tun and brewkettle
— A brewbag, size to fit your kettle
— Two plastic fermentation buckets with an airlock and a faucet
— PVC tubing for syphoning
— Scales, thermometer, hydrometer, pH test strips (or a pH meter, which is more precise but also more expensive)
— Caustic soda, acid-based sanitiser, bottle brush
— Crown caps, manual crown capper, bottles (you can easily reuse empty bottles)
— Useful items you may already have in your kitchen: measuring cup, plastic spoon, skimmer, colander…

EXTRA
— Malt mill. You can order the exact amount of milled malts online, but if you like the physical aspect of brewing, milling malts yourself is a nice workout.

Additionals for more advanced brewing
— Yeast bottle glass (e.g. to grow captured wild yeast)
— 5 litre demijohn with an airlock (e.g. to experiment with a part of your wort)

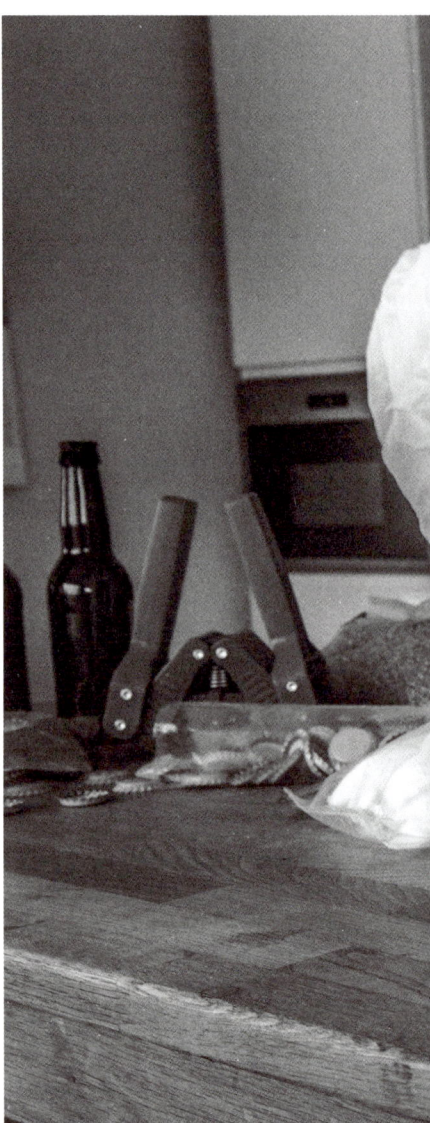

BIAB RECIPE STRUCTURE AND BASICS

Every recipe in the book is built up the same way and aims at **11 litres** in the fermenter and about **10 litres** to go into your bottles.

INGREDIENTS

— Every recipe will of course contain a list of the amount of malts, hops and yeast you need, or possible extras. You will notice that some ingredients, hops in particular, will feature repeatedly in different recipes. This wasn't a lack of inspiration, but a means to show that what's left in your freezer from a previous brew session (you hardly ever need a whole package of hops) can be used for a different beer style as well. Of all the ingredients hops are probably the most expensive, so we don't want to waste any.

MASH

- For most recipes you will **start with 16 litres of water** in a 20 litre kettle and a brewbag you will need to attach to the handles of the kettle.
- Warm up the water to the **strike temperature** in the recipe.
- Most brew in a bag recipes mention one-step mashing, which means you hold the temperature for a whole hour to extract the fermentable sugars from the malts. Some recipes include a second step to extract more non-fermentable sugars to enhance the body of the beer.
- The schedule for step mashing looks like this:

90' —— Pour in the milled malts at strike temperature. The water will drop to the desired temperature (although you may need to adjust the temperature a little bit). Then stir the malts to **avoid clumps**. This may take about 5 minutes. Once you've reached the desired temperature hold it for the number of minutes mentioned in the recipe, for instance 60 minutes. This is called a **temperature rest**. If you've got a kettle with a good lid, you can turn off the heat source. The mash will insulate itself long enough to stay in the desired temperature range for about an hour. If you want to be really sure, you can wrap a blanket around the kettle. Make sure the heat source is switched off!

85' —— Adjust **pH** to 5.4 to optimise the conversion of starch into **fermentable sugars** like maltose. You will mostly have to lower pH. The easiest way to do that for this volume is by adding calcium sulfate, lactic acid or phosphoric acid to the mash. For the right dosage read the package instructions.

30' —— If a second mash step is included, you will have to heat up the mash to 72°C (try to do this 1° per minute) and hold for 20 minutes. At this temperature starch is converted into **non-fermentable sugars** like dextrins. When heating up make sure the bag doesn't touch the bottom of the kettle.

10' —— Heat up to 78°C. This is called **mash out** and is done to end enzyme activity and makes the grainbed and wort more fluid so you can drain more wort from the grains. If you have to heat up to 78°C, starting from 63°C it will take a lot longer to do so, with a higher chance of burning the bag and caramelising the sugars. Since this is probably a beer you want to be dry, with a lighter malt bill that will drain easier and faster, you can skip this phase without affecting the final result.

FROM MASH TO BOIL

— Pull out the bag, let it **drain**. Don't squeeze it. The grainbed contains a lot of tannins that may give unwanted flavours to your beer.
— You should be able to **start the boil with 15 litres** of wort. If more wort is needed, put the bag in a second kettle and sparge with water at 80°C (sparging is not necessary when you brew in a bag, but may be helpful if you want more wort to start the boil). Add the extra wort to the main kettle until you have 15 litres.
— Measure the wort's **pre-boil original gravity**. The desired pre-boil gravity is mentioned in every recipe. Specific gravity is calibrated at 20°C, but your wort will be a lot warmer. An online calculator will help to recalculate the correct gravity (see Useful websites).

BOIL

70' —— Start to boil the wort. Adjust pH to 5.2 to enhance protein flocculation.

60' —— Boil for 60 minutes. Add **bittering hop**.

10' —— Add 3 grams of **Irish moss** (the same amount in every recipe). This seaweed makes proteins, which make your beer cloudy, clump together and drop to the bottom, so you can easily separate them from the wort you transfer to the fermenter.

15'–00' —— Add **hops for flavour and aroma**. The longer your hops boil the more the alpha acids in the hops will influence the bitterness. The shorter the hops boil the more the other components, like humulene and myrcene, will have an influence on flavour and (eventually) aroma. This of course also depends on the hop variety used.

00' —— Stop the boil.

FERMENTATION

— **Cool down the wort** to 25°C. You can use a wort chiller (add it to the boil 5 minutes before the end to sterilise it) or put the kettle in a sink filled with ice water.
— Measure the **original gravity** of the wort: you're measuring the amount of solids, mostly sugar, in the water. If you end up a bit higher than the recipe says, you can add cool mineral water from an unopened bottle.
— Syphon to the fermentation bucket using a PVC tube.
— With this method and these recipes about 11 litres should go into the fermentation bucket (you've lost about 6 litres while mashing and boiling, and added some water along the way).
— **Sprinkle the dry yeast over the wort**. You can make a yeast starter, but for homebrewing most yeasts do just fine when pitched in their dry form.
— Let it ferment for a week at the desired temperature (until there is no fermentation activity noticeable any more).
— **Measure final gravity**. The difference between the original gravity (OG) and the

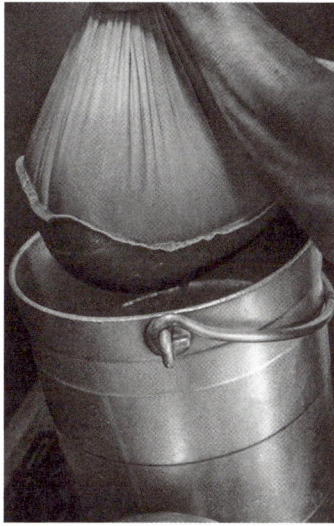

On top of a 30-litre fermentation bucket I also use a 5-litre demijohn to experiment.

A blanket (borrowed from my children) to insulate the mash kettle. This way you can keep the mash at the desired temperature for about an hour with the stove turned off.

To measure is to know. Yes, it's a cliché. But if you want to know why you get drunk so easily (or not at all) from your own beer, a hydrometer is an indispensable instrument.

final gravity (FG) is the basis to measure the amount of alcohol. You can do the maths yourself — (FG−OG) × 131.25 = % ABV — or you can use an online calculator (see Useful websites).

LAGERING AND DRY-HOPPING

— Transfer the beer (it has become beer now) to another fermentation bucket, now called the… **lagering** bucket.
— **Don't transfer the sediment**. It mainly consists of flocculated yeast cells. You will lose a litre or two at this stage.
— This stage is the most suited for **dry-hopping**. I usually put the hops in a hopbag, just like I do during the boil. This way you don't need to filter the beer or lift the hops out of it with a skimmer (this might work with whole hop cones, but can't be done when you've used pellets). Adding hops directly to the beer will give more aroma and flavour, but using a larger amount of hops in a bag will do the trick too.
— On average let the beer lager for another week in a cooler place. Some beers — such as pilsners and lagers, stouts and fruit beers — might need some more time to lager.
— The aim of lagering is to make the beer clearer and to allow certain unwanted flavours and aromas (mostly from yeast activity) to fade or disappear.

BOTTLING AND BOTTLE CONDITIONING

— Boil 7–8 g of sugar per litre in a small amount of water. Let it cool down to 25ºC and add the sugar water to the beer. This is called **priming**. Gently stir it with a sanitised spoon (don't use wooden spoons).
— Don't forget to close the lid. If you think the water inside the airlock might get sucked in, loosen the lid a bit. This might let unwanted oxygen inside the bucket, but it's better than letting the water from the airlock (which has been inside the airlock for at least two weeks) spoil your beer.
— You're ready to start bottling now. Don't forget to **sanitise the bottles** first (use a caustic soda for dirty, used bottles and an acid-based no-rinse sanitiser for clean bottles).
— Don't bottle the beer at the bottom of the bucket, because of the sediment. Again, you might lose between approximately half a litre and a litre at this stage.
— You should finally have 8–10 litres of beer or 24–30 bottles of 33 cl.
— Put the bottles in a warm dark place for (at least) a week in order to **carbonate** the beer (imperial stouts and other high-gravity beers may need more time to carbonate). Then let them rest for one or more weeks in a cooler place or a fridge.

Transferring beer with PVC tubing is a hassle, but it will lower the risk of oxidation.

USEFUL WEBSITES

Measuring temperature, pH and specific gravity are crucial in brewing. Calculating with these variables is equally important for a good result. BIAB Calculator (biabcalculator.com) and the online calculators on brewersfriend.com are very helpful tools.

'WE WANT TO CREATE BEERS THAT ARE DIFFERENT FROM WHAT WE'VE BREWED BEFORE'

DOK BREWING COMPANY

Don't Mention the War — juicy pale ale

Spacious, raw, in your face. The post-industrial looks of a polished concrete floor, red-brick walls, heavy steel beams and a high, glass-panelled saw-tooth roof. It contrasts with the crystal chandeliers suspended from that roof. They bring a hyperbolic touch of the atmosphere you would associate with the townhouses in the historical city centre. Then there are the slightly weathered wooden tables and chairs, which seem to enjoy a second life here after years of (I imagine) being crammed inside an old, barely lit pub. Lined up next to each other — in order not to feel too lost in their new, vast environment? — they invite customers to connect while enjoying a meal or a beer.

We're in Hal 16, in the Northern Docks site in Ghent. It's the playground of Dok Brewing Company, one of Ghent's newest microbreweries. The centrepiece here is a long bar with 30 taps. Above it, supported by the heavy steel beams, is a mezzanine hosting two large barrels. Behind the bar are stainless steel kettles and tanks, connected by an intricate construction of pipes.

This hall echoes the old economy, its inhabitants embody the new. It used to be filled with the transformers of the Belgian engine factory ACEC, a dinosaur of the 19th- and 20th-century industrial age. Today it is a meeting place for foodies, beer geeks and anyone who enjoys good, honest food or likes to have a beer in the sun on the large terrace outside.

The food hall with its brewpub and brewery is a fine example of how a run-down industrial building can be converted into a buzzing meeting place. It mirrors Ghent's enthusiasm for culture and taste, and the city's openness to local and artisanal entrepreneurship. The people I am about to meet here are excellent ambassadors of that spirit.

THESE BOOTS ARE MADE FOR BREWING

It's early morning when I enter Hal 16. Brewers are early birds and I will have to adapt if I want to learn the craft. The moment I step in I'm welcomed by a smoky smell. It's the scent of glowing charcoal and grilled meat. RØK, Hal 16's barbecue joint, is as yet unmanned, but a smoker is doing a slow and steady overnight job.

Janos De Baets, Dok Brewing Company's brewer and the only person present at this early hour, is already dressed for battle, wearing a T-shirt that has 'Stop drinking behind my back' written on the... back. A pun intended for customers, barflies in particular, who can read the message when Dok's bartenders are turned towards the taps while pouring a glass of beer. Janos's main weapon, though, are his rubber boots. I proudly show him mine. They're brand new, bought for the occasion, after it was stressed to me how crucial they are for a 'safe' brewing session.

Janos tells me a normal brewday starts at around 5 a.m., so what I thought was pretty early is rather late to him.

'I've already done much of the preparation, mostly sanitising, so we can start with the actual brewing. But don't worry, you'll get to do some cleaning later today,' he tells me with a smile. I have experienced at home that brewing is mostly cleaning. But at home I don't need rubber boots for that. At home the cleaning part of brewing is a lot like doing the dishes.

I wonder, will I get wet? Probably not, but I might. 'If you forget to close one of the many valves,' Janos says, pointing at the puzzling construction in front of me, 'you might lose quite a bit.' Water, wort and whatever remains of the spent grains and used hops in kettle and pipes. Janos knows what he's talking about. He tells me he's got dirty before.
But no need to worry about that for now. The first step in the brewing process is conducted far away from water. And is still far from beer. 'We'll go and get the bags of malt in our storage room. We need 175 kilos in bags of 25 kilos.' Buckle up!

THE ART OF OPENING A MALT BAG

I feel like a construction worker, hauling these 25-kilo bags up a narrow, winding staircase to the mezzanine above the bar. That's where the source of the brewing process is: the malt mill.

'Let me show you how to open these bags,' Janos tells me. What can be so difficult about that? 'They are sewn with a tiny piece of string, in such a way that the bag is airtight. If you cut the string in a particular way and you pull from left to right, the bag should be open in no time. However, it looks easier than it is. Some days it just doesn't seem to work.' A bad bag day? 'Anyway, a lot of brewers have experienced trouble opening these bags. Maybe an idea for a contest for brewers, a malt bag opening contest.'

Tossing the malt in the malt mill, bag after bag, is even more backbreaking than carrying these bags up the stairs. No need to go to the gym tonight. I will have lifted enough weight above my head as it is.

Down goes the crushed malt into the mash tun. 'Today we're brewing a juicy pale ale. Very basic, with 100% Belgian pilsner malt, and very juicy because of the hops we'll be using.' Hops are clearly Janos's thing, like for many craft brewers. The hops will spice our conversations more than once today.

'For bittering we use Magnum, probably the most used bittering hop worldwide. I like it, because it does what it needs to do: bittering, without influencing the aroma too much. That's what we'll use the other two hops for, El Dorado and Hüll Melon. That last one is German, but it's as fruity as American hops, adding notes of melon.'

He lets me sniff the freshly opened bag. The smell is, well, awesome. And in the background, indeed, a hint of melon.

'I recently met a dealer in hops who introduced me to some very interesting new hop varieties, with entirely new aromas. Our previous brew was one with HBC 472, a hop with a prominent coconut aroma.' This brown ale with a touch of coconut was named Kevin The Brown Ale, after Manchester City FC's Kevin De Bruyne, who is a Ghent native.

And while mashing is ongoing at 63°C — at this temperature carbohydrates are turned into fermentable sugars — Janos and I continue to philosophise about hops. Right next to us, in one of three stainless steel fermentation tanks, a monologue is going on. It's Kevin The Brown Ale. Or rather, CO_2 escaping from the tank through an airlock, a sign of active fermentation. It's music to a brewer's ears.

33

FIVE-MINUTE NAME GAME

Kevin The Brown Ale, Alpha Pale, 'T Is Caramelk, Trut (It's Caramilk, Bitch), My Generator Broke Down And All I Got Was This Lousy West Coast IPA, Alliet Is Groot (Alliet Is The Greatest, referring to the name of one of Dok's investors), Blond. James Blond… I can't find the usual suspects on Dok Brewing Company's tap list.

'Who comes up with these names?' I ask Janos.

'The whole crew, in fact, but we never give them much time. Five minutes is all they get,' Janos explains. 'We' refers to Janos's partners in Dok Brewing Company: beer sommelier Daniella Provost and Dimitri Messiaen, an experienced catering entrepreneur.

Dimitri has just arrived to get the dining area ready for the lunch service. He pops up behind the bar to say hello to us and is joined by Anthony, the American taproom manager and — I'm told — beer geek number one in Hal 16. Something tells me this means a lot around these people.

'I tell them something about the beer and then we start to brainstorm,' Janos continues. 'No idea is too crazy. Sometimes the brewing circumstances dictate the name, like in My Generator Broke Down And All I Got Was This Lousy West Coast IPA. Our hot water generator really broke down. But mostly it's a spur-of-the-moment idea that sticks.'

Funny and punny names for beers are definitely a craft beer thing. And the people of Dok Brewing Company have to come up with more than the average brewer, because of the high rate at which they are brewing new beers. 'We can brew up to four new beers a month. This high rate and the fact that up to now none of these beers have become regulars we sell in bottles or cans elsewhere, give us the freedom to give them crazy names. We don't have to think about branding the beers,' he tells me while pouring me a glass of U MA IS IPA (an India pale ale with a name that phonetically means 'Your mum is your dad' in the Ghent dialect and is a mild form of insult among youngsters).

It's time for an aperitif, now that lautering has started. For an ill-equipped homebrewer like myself lautering is a tricky, sometimes sticky business, and you've got your hands full with it. Here, after Janos has checked the wort's clarity, a pump does the job. So we can have a drink.

'Can you keep up with that pace?' I ask Janos, while inhaling the complex, fruity aroma of Amarillo, Citra and Mosaic in my glass. 'And what about recipes? Do you first brew a small batch?'

'I used to try things at home, but now I don't any more because it's too time-consuming. After several years at the Proefbrouwerij I became aware of how a recipe is built up. On top of that, homebrewing experience gave me a lot of insights into what (or what not) to do when creating a recipe. If you control the parameters, a lot would have to go wrong to really mess up a beer. Our advantage is that we still brew relatively small batches (1000 or 2000 litres), so the risk is limited.'

By the time this book is published, probably none of these beers will be available any longer. So no signature beer for Dok Brewing Company? 'We do have our signature styles. We do a lot of pale ales and IPAs; we like to play with porters and stouts as well. And we want to keep changing, in order not to get bored. Probably our signature is that every time you come in, you can discover something completely new.'

VARIETY IS THE SPICE OF LIFE

Variety, that's what the craft beer revolution was and is all about, a bold answer to the monotony of a lager-dominated global beer market. And it's about getting out of one's comfort zone, which applies for both brewers and consumers.

Variety also arrives on a plate today. Lunch is served by Arthur Messiaen, RØK's grill master and Dimitri's son. This month's menu contains different barbecue classics with a twist, all to be shared. There is sweet potato with olives and aioli, roasted cauliflower with curry and blue cheese, grilled sardines, pork ribs, celeriac baked in salt crust with a celeriac cream, celeriac powder and hazelnuts. And the speciality of the house: the Texas-style smoked brisket. That's the one that aromatically welcomed me this morning. Nice to finally meet — and eat — you!

To Janos there is a link between the menu of a gastronomic restaurant and his philosophy on brewing, at least in this stage of the brewery. 'A chef serves the same menu for a certain period, then he changes it. But the new menu would still be true to his style and philosophy. The same thing goes for our beers.'

I ask him whether he thinks having some regular beers, recognisable for customers, is necessary to keep a brewery afloat. 'I'm not saying we won't go for some regulars in the future. Maybe one of our customers' favourites could become a regular. But to bring it to the market would require a different commercial approach and we would have to focus on a consistent and recognisable flavour, instead of playing with the ingredients to see what comes out of the process. You know, lots of brewers put a lot of effort into branding just a couple of beers. We want to put that effort into creating many beers that are different from what we've brewed before.'

Having said this, Janos points out that Dok Brewing Company is already serving some regulars. However, these aren't Dok beers, but beers brewed by the three owners with their own microbreweries. Daniella is co-creator of L'Arogante and co-owner of the company with the same name. Dimitri runs his own gypsy brewery, The Ministry of Belgian Beer, known for its craft pilsner 13. And Janos co-founded Hedonis Ambachtsbier, known around Ghent for beers like Ouwen Duiker, Suzanne and Excuse Me While I Kiss My Stout. All of these beers are available in Hal 16's brewpub, but Daniella, Dimitri and Janos emphasise that these projects are not a part of Dok Brewing Company but separate entities co-owned by partners who are not involved in Dok (Janos in the meantime has left Hedonis Ambachtsbier to focus fully on Dok).

THE REALM OF MALTS, HOPS AND YEAST

The three met through the local beer organisation Gent Brouwt, became friends and are now business partners in what you could perceive as a long-term and formal collaboration brew or collab.

Collab. It's a recurring word in my conversations with Janos today and a key word in the minds of the new wave of craft brewers. Dok Brewing Company's kettles, tanks and pipes are running hot on collab brews these days. They are playful events among kindred spirits, fellow brewers who are equally eager to go on a quest through the realm of malts, hops, yeast and many other ingredients that might make a beer interesting, tasty and different.

About a month ago Janos was joined by Klaas and Liesbeth of Ghent's Totem brewery to brew a collab beer called Wisnia With a Cherry on Top, a so-called black forest gateau gose of 3.3% ABV. Next to the huge amount of cherries they used, it's the kettle souring technique that makes it really interesting. By adding Lactobacillus to the wort before the boil, sour flavours, usually achieved through a longer period of cask ageing, are attained in a very short time and are more easily managed and balanced. In the case of Wisnia the result is 'a liquid sour cherry pie' and it's now available on tap, a little more than a month after it was brewed. In terms of sour ales that's a Usain Bolt.

In the next couple of weeks Janos will welcome four other guests: Alvinne from the West Flemish town Moen, Northern Monk from Leeds, La Quince from Madrid and CôteWest Brewing from Lausanne.

Many brewers complain about the hassle and the lack of tangible results that come from collaboration brews, but to Janos it's a key element to keep brewing exciting. 'I work together with other craft brewers to be inspired or challenged and to learn.' These collabs are also interesting for the Dok clientele, because they aren't limited to playing around the kettles and tanks. The collaborations usually coincide with a 'tap takeover', in which the guest brewery's beers are available on Dok's taps that day.

To the new wave of craft brewers this network — which is strengthened through collabs and during beer festivals, and which is very visible on social media — also leads to the discovery of new techniques and new ingredients, hops in particular. And today I witness the network put into practice. Some guys walk into a bar... They are Americans, which is not unusual here. A lot of American tourists who visit Ghent are here for the beers too and happily stop by at Dok. But these guys are here on a mission. As it turns out, they are representatives of one of the leading hop farms in Oregon, headed for the BrauBeviale in Nuremberg, a huge trade fair for the beverage industry. Word of mouth showed them the way to Dok Brewing Company. Today they want to introduce their hop catalogue to Janos.

A CRAFT BREWER'S (DRESS) CODE

In the meantime the boil has started, the bittering hops have been added and Janos and I have emptied and cleaned the lauter tun. We drove about ten wheelbarrows of spent grains to a container outside. My rubber boots have definitely proved their worth. Tomorrow morning Janos will drop off the spent grains at a farm in a rural town on the outskirts of Ghent, where it will be used as animal feed. 'It's close to where I live, so I drop it off on my way to Dok in the morning. It's a small effort to avoid turning all this nutritious stuff into waste.'

Time for a coffee break, or rather, a break with Dok's salted caramel milk stout with vanilla. 'Tis Caramelk, Trut is tapped on nitro, and with its rich coffee and chocolate aroma and creamy mouthfeel it's perfectly tuned to the time of day. It's your strong cappuccino-with-biscuits in a glass.

'Here's another cap,' Janos says while he casually throws a green cap with the name and logo of the hop farm on the table. It lands next to his glass of Caramelk. Today he's not wearing a cap, but he usually does. It's one of those recurring elements in a craft brewer's dress code, together with the beard and the punny T-shirts. 'I only recently realised that my wardrobe is almost entirely filled with beer-related clothes,' he confesses.

Brewing is mainly cleaning. Here we are cleaning the brewery's 'hardware': stainless steel kettles, tanks, piping and valves.

Being a craft brewer is not just a job to Janos. It's a lifestyle, which not only shows in his wardrobe but also in the number of hours spent brewing and promoting the beers. 'Every craft brewer I know is a workaholic.'

HOP OD

The temperature is now okay to start fermentation. Janos has pumped the boiled wort through a plate heat exchanger to cool it down and then into the fermentation tank. Now he can add the yeast and it's my turn to do what he promised me earlier today. The words echo in my head: 'Don't worry, you'll get to do some cleaning later today!'

I'm inside the empty but hot brewkettle with my head and one arm, trying to wave off the hoppy vapour that blinds my sight and heats my nose. To no effect, however. The steam keeps on coming. I really like the aroma of hops, but this smell is so penetrating I get the impression I could OD on it.

I've released my head from the kettle and put my other arm and a hose in it to rinse the sticky hop residue from the kettle walls. I ask Janos how long it normally takes to clean the kettle. 'About a quarter of an hour,' he says, and when he notices the trouble I'm in he adds with a smile: 'Perseverance is the only thing that helps.' And so I persevere in the act of hosing until the kettle is clean enough for a more precise, chemical cleaning. It takes me, well, just a little bit longer than estimated by Janos.

And thus this brewday comes to an end for me. Janos and I will meet again tomorrow morning to drop off the spent grains at the farm. But first I will have a nice beer at home and then a good night's sleep… with dreams about endlessly carrying malt bags and cleaning out lauter tuns and brewkettles, while being dressed in nothing but hop plants of the El Dorado and Hüll Melon variety and rubber boots.

45

DOK BREWING COMPANY
—
DOKBREWINGCOMPANY.BE
HAL 16
DOK-NOORD 4B,
9000 GENT

WHAT DOES 'CRAFT BREWING' MEAN TO YOU?

Janos: 'Craft beer is beer made by small, independent breweries that are different from macro breweries in terms of innovation and creativity, and because they don't make compromises to reach their final product. The craft of making beer is key to a craft brewer, his skills are crucial. Craft brewing means that the brewer wants to distinguish himself from mass-producing breweries by putting original and authentic beers on the map. To me, a brewer is a craft brewer if he doesn't shy away from experimenting. In doing so, cooperation and collegiality with other brewers are values held in high regard.'

THE SIGNATURE BEERS OF DOK BREWING COMPANY'S PARTNERS

So far, Dok Brewing Company does not have signature beers of its own, but its partners' breweries do.

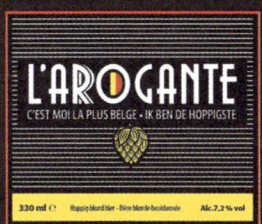

L'AROGANTE
(7.2% ABV)

'L'Arogante' is a contraction of La Roche-en-Ardenne and Ghent, the hometowns of the initial brewer and the creators of the company, and it also hints at the playful arrogance the brewers have to call their beer the hoppiest and the most Belgian of Belgians. Arrogance is not a trait usually associated with Belgians, who are (cynically) modest by reputation.

L'Arogante is an intensely hoppy golden blond with a big white creamy head. Tropical fruit from three hop varieties is prominent in the aroma. The taste at first contains a bittersweet hint of malt with spices, then finishes with lingering but gentle hop bitterness.

—

L'Arogante
larogante.be

13
(4% ABV)

It took brewers Dimitri Messiaen and Koen Van Laere 13 brews and two years to find the right recipe. They thought '13' was the perfect name for a headstrong beer, an off-centre pilsner. 13 is a light-bodied craft pilsner with a grassy hoppy nose made of Belgian pilsner malt and with Belgian hops. It tastes more bitter than malty and is in that sense the antithesis of commercial pilsners. 13 is unpasteurised and is available in three varieties: one with bottle refermentation, one without and a fresh hop version.

—

The Ministry of Belgian Beer
drink13.beer

SUZANNE
(5% ABV)

'Suzanne' refers to 'saison', a beer style favoured by Janos and his fellow brewer at the time, Leopold De Ketelaere. When they were still homebrewing, they seemed to spend more time with their saison beers than with their girlfriends. As a joke they nicknamed these beers 'Suzanne'. Later it became a satirical character who goes to war against beer marketers and so-called brewers, which unintentionally caused a bit of an uproar. Although Janos is no longer part of Hedonis Ambachtsbier he still holds Suzanne dear. Suzanne is a deep yellow, slightly hazy spelt saison, dry-hopped with Hallertau Blanc. It has a peppery aroma with fruity notes and comes in light and frizzy with some hoppy bitterness and subtle acidity, to leave slowly but with an extra dry touch, the result of using an all-consuming yeast strain.

—

Hedonis Ambachtsbier
hedonisambachtsbier.be

Kickstarting a craft beer revolution

PALE ALE

The pale ale is one of the beer styles that was revived during the craft beer revolution. The recipe I'm using here is based on the recipe of Dok Brewing Company's Don't Mention the War and is perfect to start with as a homebrewer. It's very basic and straightforward with only one type of malt.

One of the reasons pale ales are so popular among craft brewers is because they allow brewers to play with a variety of hops and hop techniques.

One of the early craft beer brewers' hop favourites was Cascade. In the 1970s, the birth decade of the American craft beer revolution, Cascade hops were a fairly new variety, grown in labs at Oregon State University to find a hop variety that was resistant to downy mildew. Cascade was released in 1972 but it wasn't very successful at first. The big industry brewers weren't keen to use it in their lagers, because the aroma and flavour were too distinctive. In 1975, however, the revitalised Anchor Brewing Company in San Francisco used Cascade for its Liberty Ale, a single hop beer that is considered to be the first modern American IPA and the first modern American craft beer.

Northwestern American homebrewers quickly followed. They wanted to brew beers that were different from the commercial beers — mainly lagers — available in supermarkets and bars. The distinctive character of the native Cascade fit the bill.

A cascade of homebrewers

America's Home Brew Act of 1979 made homebrewing, which was already quite popular 'underground', legal. The Act was an important moment in the craft beer revolution, because it allowed homebrewers 'to come out of the closet'. For many of them the next step was to become professional microbrewers.

Californian Ken Grossman was one of those early homebrewers-turned-pro. He first started with a homebrew shop in Chico, North California, but quickly expanded it to a brewery he named Sierra Nevada Brewing Company, after the nearby Sierra Nevada mountain range. One of the first beers he brewed, in 1980, was one he simply called 'Pale Ale'. It has since become iconic and is still available today — in large quantities, because Sierra Nevada has grown from a microbrewery into a craft beer giant.

As an interpretation of a classic English pale ale, which in the 1970s had become a bland and boring mass product, Sierra Nevada's Pale Ale is one of the kickstarter beers of the American craft beer revolution. And like Anchor Brewing Company's Liberty Ale, the resinous and citrusy Cascade hops are a part of its DNA.

Old World meets New World

Pale ales are not just interesting for fans of hop-forward beers, there is also interesting history behind the style. In a sense you could say that it was born in the Old World in the 18th century, travelled to the New World in the wake of English immigrants, was reinvented there in the 1970s, and since the end of the 20th century, the last ten to 20 years in particular, came back home to Europe as a global phenomenon.

The English-style pale ales as we know them from brands like Bass, on the other hand, originated in the 1800s from a local, English context: earthy, floral hops from Kent, a new type of pale malts dry roasted on coke from Northern England, and the hard, alkalic water from Burton upon Trent, England's brewing capital at the time. It was a perfect marriage resulting in a dry, refreshingly bitter and clear beer. At first intended for the upper classes, it was the antithesis of the sweet and sour, often syrupy porters and stouts of the working classes. And because of its lighter colour — amber, 'pale' only in comparison with the 'darkness' of brown ales and black porters and stouts — it was perfectly suited to being served in a glass, which in that period was quickly becoming the most popular drinking vessel.

Today pale ales come in many forms, but they share a couple of characteristics. They are dry and hoppy ales, with a very limited presence of yeasty aromas like esters, and they are fairly pale, ranging from amber to very light blond.

An Old World-New World pale ale

The recipe below is based on Dok Brewing Company's pale ale and is intended to come out as a very hoppy, fruity, extra dry and very pale ale rather low in alcohol (5–6% ABV). For practical reasons I used different hop varieties. El Dorado and especially Hüll Melon are not always available for homebrewers, so I used East Kent Goldings and Cascade instead. It was an adaptation born out of necessity, but it grew into my own modest attempt to bring a touch of beer history and some traces of the Old and the New Worlds into my homebrew pale ale.

FOR 11 LITRES PALE ALE

MALT: *2.5 kg of pilsner malt*
HOP: *14 g of Magnum, 70 g of East Kent Goldings, 70 g of Cascade*
YEAST: *SafAle US-05*
EXTRA: *Irish moss*

MASH

— Add 16 litres of water to a kettle and attach the brewbag to the handles of the kettle. Warm up the water to 65°C.

90' — Pour in the milled malts. The water will drop in temperature to about 63°C. Stir the malts to avoid clumps. Hold at 63°C for 60 minutes.

80' — Adjust pH to 5.5.

30' — Heat up to 72°C (try to do this 1° per minute) and hold for 20 minutes.

— Pull out the bag, let it drain. You should be able to start the boil with 15 litres of wort with a pre-boil original gravity of 1039.

BOIL

70' — Start to boil the wort. Just before it starts boiling adjust pH to 5.2.

60' — Boil for 60 minutes. Add Magnum (14 g).

10' — Add Irish moss.

02' — Add Kent Goldings (70 g).

00' — Stop the boil.

FERMENTATION

- Cool down the wort to 25°C.
- Measure the specific gravity of the wort. You should reach an original gravity of 1050.
- Transfer to the fermentation bucket.
- Sprinkle the dry yeast over the wort.
- Let it ferment for a week at 20–22°C.
- Final gravity should be around 1008, approximately 5.5% ABV.

LAGERING AND DRY-HOPPING

- Transfer the beer to the lagering bucket. Don't transfer the sediment.
- Dry-hop with Cascade (70 g) and let it lager for another week in a cooler place.

BOTTLING AND BOTTLE CONDITIONING

- Boil 70 g of sugar (7 g per litre) in a small amount of water. Let it cool down to 25°C.
- Remove the bags with hops from the bucket and add the sugar water. Gently stir it with a sanitised spoon. Close the lid. You're ready to start bottling.
- You should finally have 8–10 litres of beer or 24–30 bottles of 33 cl.
- Put the bottles in a warm dark place for a week in order to carbonate the beer. Then let them rest for another week in a cooler place, a cellar or a fridge. To enjoy the hop qualities of this beer, don't wait too long to drink it.

BREWING NOTES

- Fermentation didn't start well. I had to open the fermentation bucket (always a risk) and stir the wort with a sanitised spoon to activate the yeast. It worked. Later I could tell my intervention hadn't caused any infection. (The same yeast strain didn't cause a problem in other brews. Didn't I aerate enough?)
- Many manuals suggest adding yeast for bottle conditioning. I probably added a bit too much, which causes bottles to overflow and sediment to affect the hop aromas and flavours. Lesson learned: extra yeast isn't necessary for homebrewers. Because most homebrews still contain some living yeast at the moment of bottling, adding priming sugar is enough to reactivate it and build up CO_2 inside the bottle.

'I BELIEVE IN LEARNING TO LOVE NEW STYLES BY BREWING THEM'

SIPHON BREWING

Blinker — saison

'Sorry I'm a little late.' I tried to arrive at Siphon Brewing at 6 a.m. sharp and it could have worked. From home to Damme it's only a brief hour. But I didn't make it. The early brewer's hours don't come naturally to me. On top of that, I missed a small country road that would have led directly to the well-known, arcadian but remote Siphon restaurant and its brewery. 'Worth a detour' is what I read on the Gault-Millau website. Well, I took the advice to heart.

'No problem,' says head brewer Franklin Verdonck, who emerges from behind the mash tun when I put my head through the door. He has clearly been active for some time already this morning, grabbing a quick bite from a sandwich he holds in his hand. 'Hope you don't mind I started mashing in already? We've got a tight schedule.' Today I'm joining Franklin on two consecutive brew sessions. Two times 500 litres of Blinker, a saison and the restaurant's house beer on tap, which will go into a 1000 litre tank to ferment.

'They're new, these three 1000 litre fermentation tanks. As you can see they're quite large for the place.' Siphon Brewing is quite literally a micro brewery. It's housed inside a converted sheep shed — a few months before the brewery started, sheep were still grazing on the lawn in front of it. Every tank and kettle is placed in the most efficient manner now. Only the three new tanks appear to disturb the balance. They look a bit oversize in this shed — it has been well renovated, but hasn't increased in size.

The only place left to put the tanks was right in front of the only window. 'There used to be a table in front of that window where we put all sorts of stuff, such as our notes, scales or tools like a pH meter and a hydrometer to measure the wort's gravity,' Franklin tells me. And looking outside from in between two of the tanks I can tell the window holds an amazing view: pasture, rows of willows and poplars as far as the eye can see, and in the distance the canal that flows from Bruges to Sluis.

BEER AND LOVERS

'There's hardly any daylight coming through that window and the view is gone, but we mostly leave the gate open while we're brewing anyway. Still, we'll need to reorganise the place a bit in the near future.' Franklin knows what he's talking about. He knows the possibilities and limitations of the place: he assembled and installed the brewing system himself. 'It was designed and sold by an Israeli company and arrived three years ago as an IKEA type of kit from China. Every part was labelled so we knew which pipe belonged to which joint. It took me about three weeks to assemble it. It was intense. And I have to say that at times I felt fortunate to have my engineering background.'

Franklin is a qualified electrotechnical engineer who got into homebrewing more than 15 years ago and then, newly passionate about making beer, attended night school to become a beer connoisseur together with his wife Kim. One of his 'classmates' was Breandán Kearney, a former lawyer from Ireland who came to Belgium with his Belgian girlfriend and fell in love with beer too. The two started homebrewing together, soon raising their standards and trying to win the Brouwland Biercompetitie, a homebrew contest. They didn't win, but got some good feedback, which encouraged them to keep on going and caused the first spark for a professional brewing career.

Franklin takes another bite from his sandwich. 'I like a full breakfast at home, you know, cereals and fruit, but if I have to be here this early I have breakfast here, one bite at a time throughout the morning.' In the meantime Nele, the photographer, has arrived too, all eyes for the beautiful setting, enhanced by the morning sunlight. She will definitely be able to take some stunning pictures here.

I notice that Nele is wearing new white sneakers and so is Franklin. 'You've brought rubber boots?' he asks her. 'We're about to start pumping the wort to the kettle and then we'll empty the mash tun. The floor will be all wet in no time.' 'Oops, I forgot the boots,' Nele replies. She's a great documentary photographer, but breweries are a fairly new world to her. As we can tell from the spotless shoes she wears today... Fortunately, Franklin has a spare pair of rubber boots she can wear. They look a bit large on her, but they'll be useful when the cloudy water — some wort residue that is left inside the mash tun after filtering and pumping is completed, and rinse water — starts flowing all over the floor any time now.

48 HOURS

Whenever I visit a brewery I try to make myself useful, which in reality means I get to shovel the spent grains out of the mash tun and practise the art of wiping the floor. Now that sparging and pumping is done I get to play my part. I fill large baskets with the spent grains and then Franklin and I pull the heavy baskets outside, ready to be picked up by the people of Kopje Zwam (which translates as 'a cup of mushrooms'), a cooperative of mushroom farmers in Bruges. They utilise used coffee grounds as a substrate layer to grow mushrooms, and now they're testing whether spent grains can be used too.

The hot grains smell great, and together with the pleasant cold — today's a chilly but beautiful, sunny February day — it stimulates my growing appetite. Unlike Franklin I had breakfast very early and with lunchtime steadily drawing near I'm getting hungry. 'Normally, when we have guests, we have lunch in the restaurant, but it's closed. They're having their annual three-week holiday,' Franklin explains. I'll have to grab some lunch in the centre of Damme instead.

Siphon Brewing is situated on the premises of the Siphon restaurant, a four-generation family business, well known in and outside of this corner of Belgium, in between the North Sea and the Dutch border. 'Breandán got to know the family of the Siphon through a mutual contact, and they were interested in starting a brewery beside the restaurant. One thing led to another and now here we are.

Artisanal brewing can be tough. Removing the spent grains from the lauter tun is mainly done manually. Dragging the big bucket with spent grains outside is manual labour all the way.

'Working like this, in association with the restaurant, certainly gave us a head start. But still, running a brewery isn't an easy thing.' In a small brewery like Siphon Brewing doing things together and enjoying your passion is important, but doing things in an efficient way is crucial. And to get the business started Franklin had to combine two jobs. 'We used to do these marathon brew sessions from Monday morning to Tuesday night, because from Wednesday to Friday I still worked as an electrotechnical engineer.' It meant that different batches of the different beers had to be brewed within 48 hours.

Today's two consecutive batches of Blinker are like a walk in the park for Franklin. But he emphasises he's happy that the marathon brewdays are over. Franklin is a full-time brewer now. 'You can't keep on doing these marathon sessions. I'm glad I can spend all my working time on brewing now and more or less have a normal workweek.'

STORYTELLING

Franklin is now officially the head brewer of Siphon Brewing. Breandán still assists, but is now more involved in general management and planning. Breandán also works on other beer projects, like his blog and podcast *Belgian Smaak* and other beer writing, for which he has won several awards.

At Siphon Brewing, Breandán is also responsible for telling the stories of the beers. To Franklin and Breandán these stories are not just marketing tools, and they provide a lot more than mere fun. The stories are a part of the identity of the beers. Franklin: 'Every beer and its name needs to tell something about Siphon Brewing.' 1902, for instance, is a tripel with lavender and honey that reflects the link between Belgium's long beer tradition, the drive to try new things and the restaurant's history, which dates back to 1902.

Blinker is no different. It is the local nickname for the Leopoldkanaal, one of two canals that run parallel and cross the 'siphon', a large version of a plumber's trap used to level the water of the two parallel canals with the canal from Bruges to Sluis that crosses them. Both the neighbourhood's and the restaurant's names were derived from that piece of waterway construction.

I'm looking at a whiteboard on the side wall and notice a random set of notes and a brewing schedule. 'We recently forgot the copies of our brew sheet and wrote down the mashing schedule on the whiteboard. We always want to keep track of the whole process so we can compare different batches of the same beer or adjust the recipe to make it better.'

Above the notes I read: 'No shortcuts. Be unafraid', Siphon Brewing's slogan, seemingly serving as a title. It's exactly what I experience after the first hours I've spent with Franklin: he's got a clear and bold view on what beer can and should be. 'An American beer journalist once described us as "Old World meets New World", and that's exactly the type of beer we're trying to make. We like to bring classic Belgian styles with a twist, but also love to interpret international styles. Surprising beers, but always well balanced.'

Much like Blinker, I guess, which is in a way a straightforward interpretation of a more traditional saison. Franklin uses pilsner, Munich and dark wheat malts, and Challenger and Goldings hops. The yeast used is a standard saison yeast, which is eager to eat all fermentable sugars. The Siphon touch, however, is the mashing time. Like with most saisons he uses only one temperature rest, but instead of the regular 67°C, Franklin lets the mash rest at 62°C for one hour. This leads to more fermentable sugars in the wort. Combined with the all-consuming yeast, Blinker is a bone-dry, spicy, crispy, thirst-quenching ale of 5% ABV with a touch of citrus and a bit of refreshing acidity to the nose and palate from the wheat malt.

SMOKED EEL

Blinker used to be one of Siphon Brewing's core beers, but has recently been replaced by the kölsch-style Lieve and is now only available on the restaurant tap. 'We love saisons very much and we're very proud of Blinker,' Franklin says. 'It's the first beer we brewed here, but it's difficult to convince beer drinkers to try new saisons. Because many of the restaurant's clientele like the beer, we reoriented Blinker as the house beer.'

It seems to me that from a restaurant's point of view it is an excellent alternative for a pilsner and it has all the qualities to lure more traditional beer drinkers among its clientele to explore the other, more adventurous Siphon beers, some of them variations on the saison theme. Hutwe, for instance, a coffee saison 'spin-off' of Blinker. Siphon Brewing made it together with coffee roaster OR Coffee from Ghent, using coffee beans from the Hutwe washing station in the Congo, selected for their subtle acidity that blends well with the bitterness and the citrusy touch of Blinker. Or Cendre, a so-called black India saison, which embodies elements of an IPA, a stout and a saison and references in aroma, taste and name the home-smoked eel for which the restaurant is renowned.

While the Blinker is boiling we find a spot in the late winter sun not too far from the smoker that is used for that home-smoked eel. 'We got the idea for Cendre while watching the restaurant staff smoke the eels. The smell is amazing. And we really like the artisanal approach. It's how we like to make beers as well.'

Franklin and I are joined by Mathias De Stecker, who's responsible for the sales and marketing strategy of Siphon Brewing. It's noon. Time to taste a Siphon beer before I go grab a bite in Damme. Franklin digs up an older bottle of Blinker and demonstrates how hoppy beers don't have a long shelf life. 'The sooner you drink hoppy beers the better.' Not that the older Blinker is bad beer, but it has lost its character, as I can tell when comparing it to a sip from a recent bottle. The hop point is made loud and clear a glass later, when I have a taste from a recently bottled Damme Nation, a Belgian-style IPA abundant in fruity and floral hops. A nice display of both richness and balance in aroma and flavour.

Lieve, one of Siphon Brewing's core beers. It's a kölsch-style light beer and the brewers' first, cautious step into the world of German beer styles.

BABY

When I get back from lunch Franklin has already finished the whirlpool and cooled down the boiled wort. He is about to transfer the first batch to the fermentation tank. He'll soon be able to start the second batch. 'One of the advantages of doing two batches in a row is that you don't have to CIP [Clean-In-Place with chemicals] the kettles and pipes. A good rinse will do.' And for a microbrewery it's also a way to allow growth while still using a smaller installation.

While the brewing installation may still be the same, Siphon Brewing added these three new 1000 litre fermentation tanks to the six 500 litre tanks already in place from the start. Not only do they allow larger batches to be produced — Siphon Brewing brews some 55 hectolitres per month, which is 16,000 bottles or 270 kegs — these larger fermentation tanks are also more efficient. The conical form of a tank helps to collect trub and sediment in the cone, so the beer that is pumped to a bright beer tank — from which the beer is bottled — is clear. The remaining content is then flushed down the drain: a necessary loss of at least 25 litres per tank, whether that's a 500 litre or a 1000 litre tank. Only, the 'share' of this loss is much smaller in the 1000 litre tank.

Siphon Brewing's steady growth is carefully welcomed by Franklin. There is this matter of efficiency and viability. After all, craft brewing isn't done in some economic vacuum. But I sense some hesitation in his voice as well. 'Demand from abroad is also increasing, but we want to keep a good balance between export and beer for the local market. At all times we want to be able to keep in touch with the people who drink our beers.

'You know, you like your baby to grow up, but you've got to beware not to grow too quickly or to become too large. At some point we will need to hire people and I won't find it easy to leave brewing to someone else. I'm a real perfectionist, especially when it comes to brewery hygiene. Inevitably I will have to leave some parts of the brewing process to future members of the crew. But we'll make sure we know very well who joins the team through thorough screening and internships.'

This growth certainly is a fine reward for three years of consistent work on a set of beers that reflects a clear philosophy and identity. As were some awards the brewery won last year. Siphon Brewing was named Best New Brewery in Belgium 2017 at the RateBeer Awards in Portland, Oregon, in January 2018. And at the World Beer Awards the label of Zwaluw, Siphon's rye session ale, was the country winner for World's Best Label Design 2017. 2018 definitely was a golden year for Siphon Brewing.

BEER ENGINEER

'And in fact, for me it all started with making wine. Like my father I made elderflower wine, but as with any type of wine your influence on the process is limited, so I started making beer instead. As a brewer you've got a bigger impact on the final product.' The engineer in Franklin is never far away. 'With beer you've got so many possibilities with only four ingredients.'

You could say that Franklin is willingly following one of the oldest government limitations on a brewer's 'creativity', the Reinheitsgebot, which was instigated in Bavaria in 1516 in order to keep brewers from being creative for the wrong reasons: messing around with cheaper or fewer ingredients to make more profit. 'I love the creativity such limitations stimulate, but I understand that German brewers got fed up with the Gebot after 500 years.'

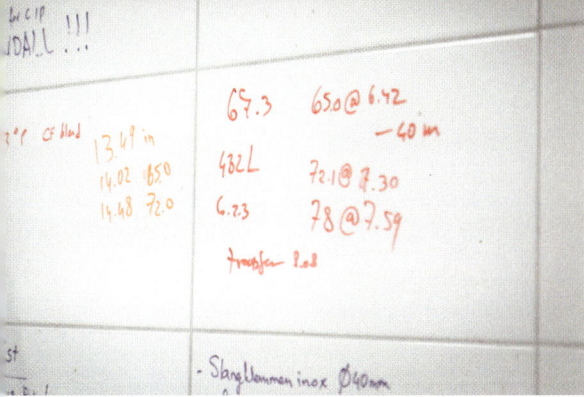

Franklin is not the only craft brewer who loves to play with less to gain more. Early on in the craft beer revolution American craft brewers brewed all-grain beers according to the Reinheitsgebot as an act of opposition against the big industry breweries, who use adjuncts like corn in their lagers and pilsners as a cheap alternative for malt.

And like many craft brewers he has recently embraced some German styles of beer. Kölsch, for instance, a hybrid between an ale and a lager, because of the way in which the ale yeast is used: instead of fermenting at higher temperatures, commonly between 15 and 25°C, the beer ferments in temperatures below 15°C, much like a lager. The result is an ale with subtle fruitiness but without prominent esters, and with more space for delicate hop aromas and flavours to surface. 'Breandán is not a fan of German-style beers, but with the kölsch he became more convinced to be open to it.

'My wife Kim and some friends have recently brewed a hefeweizen. It is fermenting as we speak. Here, I'll let you taste it.' Franklin pours a small glass straight from the tank. 'You can see how hazy it is. Fermentation is nearly finished, but the yeast will remain in suspension like this, even in the final product.' *Hefe* means 'yeast' in German and *Weizen* is 'wheat', both ingredients that lead to a hazy beer and typical characteristics like aromas of banana and clove.

In January 2019 Franklin's wife Kim van Opdurp (Zytholicious) united her friends Katrien Bruyland (Epicuralia), Daniella Provost (Dok Brewing Company) and Leen Geers (Geers Beer store) to brew a beer to celebrate International Women's Day. Brewing is still widely considered to be 'a man thing' and Kim and co. felt it was about time to show that women also know how to brew.

They named their beer Nola, the female form of St Arnoldus, patron saint of brewing, and chose an easy to drink German weizen of 5% ABV as a canvas to play with hops like Belma. Its fruity aromas and flavours — melon and peach — are complementary with the subtle banana esters from the traditional German ale yeast.

CELEBRATION

'And here's another one you need to taste.' Franklin pours a glass from another fermentation tank. 'I'm not really a fan of kettle souring myself. I have never tasted a kettle soured beer that can stand up to barrel soured beer. But I believe in learning to love new styles by brewing them.

'This one we've brewed in collaboration with Tempel Brewery from Sweden and Brasserie de Blaugies for our Noble Gas project. It's a series of six collabs we're doing to celebrate our third anniversary.' (The beers were released on 29 June 2019 at Siphon Brewing's anniversary party and were distributed on a small scale in six-packs containing a bottle of each collab beer.)

It seems like Siphon Brewing has a lot to celebrate. And now that we can transfer the second batch of Blinker to the fermentation tank, I can also think about celebrating the end of an inspiring brewday. I'll be willingly tempted by a local mermaid, calling from a pond I can see through that one window, from in between two 1000 litre fermentation tanks. Cassandra is calling and she brings with her a promise of invigorating coffee, sensual dark chocolate and a kiss from the sea.

WHAT DOES 'CRAFT BREWING' MEAN TO YOU?

Franklin: 'What does "craft" mean? To me it's a term that says a lot and nothing at the same time. Does it have to do with the volume of beer produced or the quality of the beer? Or the way the brewer perceives the world of beer and beer styles? I think "craft" is more about the passion a brewer needs to have to be able to deal with beer and brewing day in, day out. About how much he values the raw materials he works with and the amount of respect he pays to tradition. But it is also about being open to new beer trends. And probably the most important element: craft brewing is about respecting the beer consumer. But then again, this says a lot and nothing at the same time. Just like the term "craft".'

SIPHON BREWING

SIPHONBREWING.BE
DAMSE VAART-OOST 1,
8340 DAMME

THE SIGNATURE BEERS OF SIPHON BREWING

Siphon Brewing brews classic Belgian beers with a twist, inspired by international styles. This idea clearly translates into their signature beers, which are a creative interpretation of the archetypal Belgian threesome: blond, amber and dark. The selection Franklin made to represent Siphon Brewing's identity consists of a blond yeast-forward, an amber hop-forward and a dark malt-forward beer, none of them very high in alcohol.

LIEVE
(4.5% ABV)

Lieve is a kölsch-style beer named after the canal that flowed from Ghent to Damme and was partly responsible for the latter city's economic importance during the late Middle Ages.
Lieve is brewed with pilsner malt only and is hopped with Citra and Mandarina Bavaria. It appears as a light golden blond and is a refreshing, lively carbonated hop-bitter beer. It nicely blends the aromas and flavours of the three key ingredients brewers love to play with — the fruitiness of the hops, some gentle maltiness and subtle esters from the yeast — only to surprise you with a lingering bitter finish.

DAMME NATION
(7% ABV)

Damme Nation is an IPA that brings together distinctive elements from three (India) pale ale traditions: British, Belgian and American. Its amber colour goes back to the beginning days of pale ales and IPAs in 19th-century England, its subtle caramel notes refer to a Spéciale Belge, and its hop profile — with Amarillo, Cascade and Citra — is clearly modern American.
To the nose Damme Nation has a prominent hoppy character with hints of grapefruit, pine and grass, and a tiny touch of apple. Similar flavours, complemented with some spices and caramel, are supported by a malty backbone.

CASSANDRA
(7% ABV)

This oyster stout is pitch black, with a creamy, beige head — coffee with milk — and for only 7% ABV it is abundant in aromas and flavours. And as the substyle name suggests, oysters, or more precisely oyster shells from the Siphon restaurant, are used as an ingredient during the boil.
The aroma is mainly that of roasted malts, but some fruitiness is surfacing as well. Cassandra, named after a mermaid from local legend, has a creamy mouthfeel. The palate is dominated at first by a roasted, coffee-like character, followed by a touch of sweet, dried fruits, some licorice and a tiny bit of dark chocolate. A very distant hint of minerality close to saltiness is also present — the brewers poetically describe it as 'sea-kissed'. The finish is gently bitter from the roasted malts.

The hoppiest

INDIA PALE ALE

If there is any beer style that epitomises the scope of the craft beer revolution, it's the IPA or India pale ale. It was one of the first American beer styles to break away from the monotonous lager-dominated market and, much like lagers, you can find it in all shapes and sizes all over the world. Because of their popularity IPAs have also been adopted by the big industry brewers, but so far that only seems to spur craft brewers to be evermore creative with the style and come up with new variations on the IPA theme again and again.

Popular history tells that IPAs were 'invented' by George Hodgson of London's Bow Brewery at the end of the 18th century to better preserve beer on the sea voyage to Britain's colony India.

Historical reality, however, is more complex and the 'birth' of the IPA can't be pinned down to one specific moment in time. Hoppy beers were already becoming popular in Britain, and London in particular, before they were sent to India. October ales from the countryside, for instance.

Hodgson should be credited for his business instinct, though. He made good money with the export of beer to India at the end of the 18th century. Because he gave his neighbours of the East India Company a credit line of 18 months, the company mostly bought beer from Bow Brewery, porter at first and from 1822 on also the strongly hopped October ale. But when Hodgson's sons took over the brewery and started to exploit their near-monopoly the East India Company engaged the Allsop brewery from Burton upon Trent to brew a pale ale like the October ale. Allsop used a lighter kind of malt — white malt — and the local hard water, which resulted in a beer of better quality. Other Burton brewers, like the later giant Bass, quickly followed the example of Allsop.

Their hoppy pale ales were shipped to India, but were never as succesful as porters and stouts, which always made up the greater proportion of beer consumed by British soldiers and expats in India, although with more hops added for preservation.

Like today, the distinction between an India pale ale and a pale ale was rather arbitrary and the use of the name originated in marketing more than in actual brewing, as brewers began to present the IPA as the beer for the gentry. Sounds familiar?

Hoppy, hoppier, hoppiest

The modern American craft IPA was born in 1975 at the Anchor Brewing Company in San Francisco. Craft beer pioneer Fritz Maytag had taken over the near defunct Anchor Brewing Company, famous for its Anchor Steam beer, in 1965. Maytag wasn't a brewer and had to learn the craft, but did so passionately and patiently.

It wasn't until 1971 that he sold the first batch of Anchor Steam. In 1975 he released Liberty Ale, an English-style single hop pale ale in which he used Cascade, at the time a fairly new American hop variety, for bittering and dry-hopping. Today Liberty Ale is called the first modern American IPA.

Anchor's Liberty Ale wasn't just the first step in making outstanding American craft beers, it was also the start to brew ever hoppier beers and to keep on 'inventing' new substyles of the IPA.

Stone Brewing's Arrogant Bastard Ale, with 100 International Bitterness Units (IBUs), based on an accidental miscalculation of the amount of hops and well marketed afterwards, has turned into a classic among very hop-bitter beers, although it certainly is far from the hoppiest. Some brewers have tried to go all the way up to 1000 IBUs (which technically isn't possible), either intentionally or unintentionally turning the IBU race into a gimmick.

Then there's more to say for hoppy beers that aim for complexity. Russian River Brewing Company's Pliny the Elder, for instance, the first commercialised DIPA or double IPA, and Pliny the Younger, a triple IPA only available on tap in Santa Rosa, California, because of its complex and fragile hop characteristics with only a short shelf life.

DIPA, TRIPA, West Coast IPA, Imperial IPA, Black IPA, sour IPA, Brett IPA, Grapefruit IPA, Brut IPA and… Belgian IPA. Seems like a lot of name dropping. There are quite a lot of differences, though, within recurring IPA features, and brewers and consumers alike use the style names to navigate through the huge number of beers that are brewed and released every day. New names are invented all the time, which may be confusing, or just more hype, but it also shows the dynamics within the craft beer world.

Hopping

The quest for hoppier beers and more complex hop aromas goes hand in hand with the development of hopping techniques, the purpose being to extract the maximum amount of flavours and aromas from the hops.

There is dry-hopping of course. And continual hopping, used by Sam Calagione of Dogfish Head Craft Brewery in his 60, 90 and 120 Minute IPAs. Inspired by a television cooking show, Calagione adds small portions of hops throughout the boil to enhance hop complexity. Dogfish Head Craft Brewery, based in Delaware, also came up with the Randall, a double-chamber filter connected to a tap so the beer will flow through fresh hops when tapped.

Craft beer pioneer Sierra Nevada uses a hop torpedo for its Torpedo Extra IPA. The torpedo is a cylindrical tank in which beer circulates through a perforated cylinder with whole-cone hops. Variations are the hop rocket and the hop gun.

A logical way to improve hop quality is to start at the basis, by either processing hops differently — wet hops (canned hops containing undried oils) or Cryo Hops (freeze-dried aromatic hop powder) — or more quickly, like the 24-hour hops procedure that allows the processing of hops from the field into pellets within 24 hours, limiting the loss of flavour and aroma components along the way.

Belgian-style or tripel IPA

One thing I have learned from the Belgian craft brewers I visited is that, however much they may be inspired by the American craft beer revolution, they always want to pay their respects to local tradition, for instance by bringing some local elements to an international beer style. For the IPA, that means they'll use Belgian hops instead of the strong aromatic American ones. Or they'll use a different yeast strain, like a Belgian ale yeast. That's what I tried in this tripel IPA: to bring together the fruity aromas from an American and a strongly aromatic European hop variety with the fruity esters from a Belgian ale yeast.

FOR 11 LITRES (TRIPEL) IPA

MALT: *3.6 kg of pilsner malt, 250 g of flaked oats, 300 g of Munich*
HOP: *15 g of Brewer's Gold, 100 g of Mandarina Bavaria, 100 g of Amarillo*
YEAST: *Belgian Ale Yeast M41*
EXTRA: *Irish moss, 300 g of granulated sugar*

MASH

— Add 16.5 litres of water to a kettle and attach the brewbag to the handles of the kettle. Warm up the water to 64°C.

90' —— Pour in the milled malts. The water will drop in temperature to about 62°C.
Hold at 62°C for 60 minutes. Gently keep on stirring the malts.

80' —— Adjust pH to 5.4.

30' —— Heat up to 72°C and hold for 10 minutes.

10' —— Heat up to 78°C.

— Pull out the bag, let it drain. You should be able to start the boil with 15 litres of wort with a pre-boil original gravity of 1057.

BOIL

70' —— Start to boil the wort. Just before it starts boiling adjust pH to 5.2.

60' —— Boil for 60 minutes. Add Magnum (15 g).

10' —— Add Irish moss and 300 g of granulated sugar.

00' —— Add Mandarina Bavaria (30 g) and Amarillo (30 g). Stop the boil.

FERMENTATION

— Cool down the wort to 25°C.
— Measure the specific gravity of the wort. You should reach an original gravity of 1078.
— Transfer to the fermentation bucket. Sprinkle the dry yeast over the wort.
— Let it ferment for a week at 20–25°C. Final gravity should be around 1008, approximately 9% ABV.

LAGERING AND DRY-HOPPING

— Transfer the beer to the lagering bucket.
— Dry-hop with Mandarina Bavaria (70 g) and Amarillo (70 g) and let it lager for another week in a cooler place.

BOTTLING AND BOTTLE CONDITIONING

— Boil 80 g of sugar (8 g per litre, we want fairly high carbonation) in a small amount of water. Let it cool down to 25°C.
— Remove the bags with hops from the bucket and add the sugar water. Gently stir it with a sanitised spoon. Close the lid. You're ready to start bottling.
— Put the bottles in a warm dark place for a week in order to carbonate the beer. Then let them rest for another week in a cooler place or a fridge.
— To fully enjoy the hoppy character of this beer, don't wait too long to drink it. If you let it rest a little longer the hop aroma and flavour will become less prominent, making this beer more like a complex tripel than a tripel IPA. But that shouldn't be a bad thing, should it?

BREWING NOTES

— Very lively fermentation, resulting in a final gravity lower than expected, 1006 instead of 1008, good for about 9.5% ABV. Because I wanted to test this beer at a party I needed a larger volume and brewed two batches in a row on two consecutive brewdays. The first batch was already fermenting quite actively when I added the second. I probably gave the fermentation process a boost by doing this.
— In my first version of this recipe I was more cautious with dry-hopping, using 50 g instead of 70 for each hop variety. It came out as a good Belgian-style tripel, but the hop aromas were overruled by the esters. Maybe you should be the hoppiest and go for 100 g of Mandarina Bavaria and 100 g of Amarillo?

'WE BLEND INTUITIVELY, USING ONLY OUR NOSES AND PALATES'

'T VERZET

Oud Bruin and Oud Bruin Strawberry — Flanders brown

For the previous two chapters I joined a brewer on a brewday. It was exciting and I was able to pick up good, practical ideas for my homebrews. Apart from the size of the brewing installation and the complicated set of pipes and valves, I had the impression I knew what was going on and what (limited) part I could play. Today I'm joining Alex Lippens and Koen Van Lancker of brewery 't Verzet (which translates as 'The Resistance') in Anzegem, a town in the southwestern part of Flanders. And today we won't brew.

't Verzet produces a wide range of beers, inspired by international trends but always on the solid basis of regional tradition. It first made a name as a craft brewery in Belgium and abroad with Rebel Local, a tripel-style strong blond with Belgian hops.

Today Alex and Koen will add 250 kilos of strawberries to 1000 litres of Oud Bruin, their version of a Flanders brown, a sour brown ale of mixed fermentation with a deep red-brown colour. It's quite like a Flanders red and has a long history in this part of Flanders. Alex and Koen will also blend a new batch of Oud Bruin.

I arrive shortly after the lunch break and I've missed the brewing part of their day by an inch. 'While I was finishing a batch of Super NoAH, Alex has already selected some barrels and foeders from which we'll take samples to blend,' Koen tells me. 'But we'll start with the Oud Bruin Strawberry.'

Koen guides me into a conditioned storage room with some bright beer tanks. In the middle of the room a lot of cardboard boxes are stacked. They are also somewhere in the middle of giving in to gravity. Alex is already there. He points at the boxes. 'Here they are, 250 kilos of Belgian strawberries. They're frozen, because at this time of year [February] we can't get any fresh Belgian strawberries,' Alex explains. 'They've already started melting. The strawberries are in vacuum bags, but still, some juice might drip from the boxes. Would you mind helping me carry the boxes to the barrel and foeder room?'

ROCKSTAR HALL OF FAME

Entering a foeder and barrel hall is a thrilling experience, especially for a beer geek — and regardless of the cardboard box in my hands. One is hardly ever welcomed by a musty smell, but that's not the case when you enter a hall full of wooden barrels and foeders. It's a counterintuitive sign of good health. They need a humid environment in order to keep them from leaking. I feel like I'm in a giant cellar. Looking at four foeders containing 4000 litres each only adds to this impression. They are lying one next to the other, brotherly, in unison. To the eye it's as if they're playing a simple but harmonious chord. At night, would they lead the choir of 74 other, smaller barrels? Singing something like 'Hey! Ho! Let's go!' to urge the Lactobacilli in their microbiological pogo?

If the brewing hall is the meticulously monitored and steadily beating heart of a brewery, then the foeder and barrel room is much like the extremities of our body, which respond — sometimes in odd ways — to external stimuli. Cold winter hands that start to glow in warm water, an electric shock when you hit your elbow, the blood that flows through the vessel between your legs when aroused... Quite exciting, precisely because it's hard to keep it fully under control.

Hey! Ho! Let's go! — all the barrels at 't Verzet are named after famous artists so they can be identified more easily.

I have no idea whether Alex and Koen had this comparison in mind when they added a touch of arousal, a bit of sex and drugs and rock 'n' roll to the foeder and barrel hall. No! Don't get me wrong. There are no posters of naked women on the walls (at least not where I can see them). No, the idea is in the foeders and the barrels. Inside, where the microbiological magic happens, as well as written on the foeders and barrels, which are named after Alex and Koen's favourite sex, drugs and rock 'n' roll protagonists: musical heroes both dead and alive. Bon Scott, Bob Marley, Eddie Vedder and the likes are immortalised on barrels containing ageing Oud Bruin. And on the big 4000 litre fellas, named after the four Ramones.

'There's a reason for it. It's a way to remember which barrel we used for which blend,' Koen tells me. 'First we started with Roman numerals, but we didn't study long enough to keep that idea going,' he adds ironically. 'We started using the names of our favourite artists instead.' It has turned out much like a rockstar hall of fame in its own right.

Alex tells me the idea took off a couple of years ago at a festival: 'We served Oud Bruin from single barrels and did a tasting. One barrel, nicknamed Lemmy after Motörhead's late frontman, stood out. Maybe people liked it because of the name?' 'Or because it was the oldest Oud Bruin at the time,' Koen corrects.

SUMMER IN FEBRUARY

With all the boxes put in place right next to a stainless steel 1000 litre tank, we're nearly ready to add the strawberries. Koen is filling it with CO_2 to get rid of the oxygen inside the tank. 'We do this to prevent the formation of acetic acid, which would make the beer sour in the wrong way.'

In the meantime photographer Nele has arrived and today she has brought her own rubber boots. I didn't tell her we were going to infuse Oud Bruin with strawberries today, so what are the odds… she's wearing boots with a… strawberry print.

Alex and I start opening the boxes and take out blue vacuum bags filled with ice-cold strawberries. Koen has stepped up a ladder and I hand him the bags after I've cut them open. I'm trying to keep up with him, but in my rush I force a bag to burst open, spilling strawberries all over the concrete floor. When Alex's father, Jean, pops in, I'm glad there's an extra hand.

Tempo goes up now and while I gasp for breath, in order to keep up the appearance of being a worthy assistant, Koen and Alex still find the time to make a joke or two. 'They're brewers,' Jean reacts, 'they have a screw loose and it won't be tightened any time soon.'

250 kilos of strawberries, that's a lot of boxes.

Jean is a retired construction worker and gives a helping hand in the brewery almost every day. 'In the morning I'm the first to arrive,' he tells me while fluently cutting open strawberry bags and handing them to his son, who has joined Koen on top of the tank, using a second ladder. 'This morning I was here at 6 a.m. to prepare some orders. And earlier this week, when they wanted to start brewing at 5 a.m., I arrived at 4 to warm up the water so they could start mashing in right away. I'm always awake very early, so I might as well do something useful,' he says with a smile and then quickly adds: 'But I don't start mashing. That I leave to them.'

A free extra hand is always welcome when you start a business. 'When we first started and didn't have a bottling machine yet, we bottled manually together with our dads,' Koen says. They didn't have a budget to hire people for that, so it really made a difference.

'I can't say I was very enthusiastic about Alex's plans to become a brewer,' Jean stresses. 'I still remember the day he came home from school, 18 years old, and told me and my wife he had decided what he would study after secondary school. "I'm going to be a brewer," he said and I replied there wasn't a real future in that line of business. But he was determined. "Dad," he said, "people have been drinking for centuries. They're not going to quit all of a sudden."'

Alex started studying biochemistry in Ghent, where he was one of three who majored in brewing sciences. The other two were Koen and Joran Van Ginderachter. The threesome had to work closely together in laboratory classes and became good friends. After they graduated they started working in different breweries. With less time to meet than before they started homebrewing together in order to keep their friendship alive. From homebrewing they moved to gypsy brewing, brewing the beers for their newborn beer company Brouwers Verzet during weekends at breweries De Ranke and Toye.

In 2016 Alex and Koen found investors, moved to establish a genuine brewery and changed the name to 't Verzet. Joran, who had interned in the United States, following in the footsteps of his uncle Peter Bouckaert who worked at New Belgium in Colorado, pursued his American dream. He is currently starting up his own brewery in Atlanta, called Halfway Crooks Brewing and Blending.

NOSTALGIA IN A BOTTLE

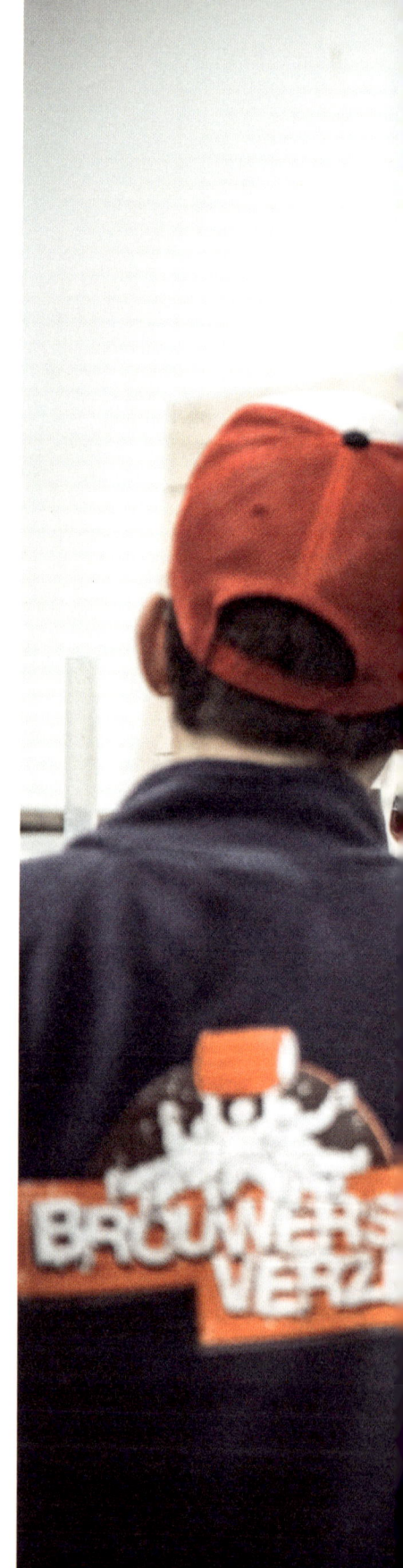

The tank is filled with strawberries now. Koen connects a hose to the bottom of the tank to pour in the Flanders brown. 'We add the beer from the bottom up to avoid oxidation.' It takes about 15 minutes for the tank to fill completely. I climb up a ladder to take a look and can't resist putting my head inside the tank. The strawberry aroma is sublime. We're in February but to my nose it's summer all-over.

While Koen finishes the strawberry infusion, Alex is busy taking samples from one of the foeders and from a series of barrels he has selected earlier today. The samples are collected in tasting glasses. Alex first pulls a nail from the front of a barrel. A tiny stream of beer flows from the nail-sized hole. 'We don't take samples from the top of the barrel, because we don't want to disturb the flor, a thin, foamy layer of wild yeast that protects the beer from oxidation and Acetobacter, the bacteria that produce acetic acid in the presence of oxygen.'

Alex puts the samples on top of an unused, square stainless steel tank. It serves as an improvised bar. He covers the glasses with beer coasters on which he has written the names of the barrels and the date of barrelling. An illustrious line-up is getting ready for showtime: Bon Scott, Michael Jackson, Bob Marley, Johnny Rotten, Joey Ramone, James Brown and 2Pac.

'These last two contain the youngest version of Oud Bruin,' Alex tells me. The James Brown barrel was filled with brown ale on 15 November 2018, only three months ago, 2Pac's was filled on 4 September. 'They're still evolving, like adolescents, with quite a bit of caramel aroma and flavour from the malts, traces of the unevolved brown ale.'

Koen has brought us a glass from the fresh brown ale to get an idea of the original aromas and flavours. It tastes a bit dull and it would not make an interesting beer in its own right. I'm impressed by how much effect barrel souring has. And by the amount of knowhow and confidence Alex and Koen have in the evolutionary capacities of this brown ale.

'We select barrels with beer aged between at least eight months and two years. It's only after eight months that the first effects of barrel ageing become prominent.'

Bob Marley is the oldest barrel, having been filled two years ago, on 22 February 2017. The tannins are pretty obvious and I can sense the need for blending here. Because of the tannins and the strong acidity Bob Marley makes for interesting beer, but it's a bit harsh. The purpose of blending is to make the final sour brown more balanced and round. How balanced and round, how prominent the acidity, is a matter of taste and the identity the brewer wants to give to his beer. 't Verzet's Oud Bruin is a no-compromise version of the style, more sour and complex than many other examples of this type of beer around the region.

It is not the only aspect in which Oud Bruin is different from other Flanders browns. Traditional Flanders browns are 'infected' with a cocktail of wild yeasts like Brettanomyces and bacteria like Lactobacillus before they enter a second stage of fermentation in stainless steel tanks. Oud Bruin in that sense is more similar to Flanders reds, which undergo a similar type of second fermentation in foeders or wooden barrels. (But to be honest, the terms Flanders brown, red or red-brown ale are often used interchangeably.) On top of that the beer is unfiltered and unpasteurised, very unusual for beers of mixed fermentation.

A poster on which the whole production process of Oud Bruin is depicted hangs above the tank, which today serves as an improvised bar. It shows visitors — like me — how, but also why, 't Verzet is making Oud Bruin the way they do. 'We brew this style of beer because we really like it, but we also want to conserve it and make it popular again. We want to bring it to a younger audience,' Koen says. One of the images on the poster, which is also on the Oud Bruin label, is an old man dressed in caricaturesque hip-hop-style clothing. He hyperbolically stands for the fusion of what's considered to be outdated on the one hand and hip on the other.

'In a way we make Oud Bruin out of a sense of nostalgia. From the stories we heard from our dads and uncles we gather that the Flanders browns they drank must have been more sour than what is mostly available today,' Alex explains. Their effort to bring back a touch of the oudbruin of old has been rewarded. In 2018 a test panel of the Flemish daily newspaper *Het Nieuwsblad* listed Oud Bruin as the second best Flanders red ale in the country, marking it 8.5/10. And Oud Bruin Oak Leaf, further aged on oak leaves, was elected number one with a 9/10.

INTUITIVE BLENDING

Alex and Koen start smelling and tasting the other samples. I try to join them, but I'm already glad I can recognise some of the aromas and flavours they point out. They don't need extensive tasting to find the right balance. Bon Scott has been shortlisted for its herbal notes, Michael Jackson will add a bready touch, a large portion will be for Joey Ramone, and either Bob Marley or Johnny Rotten will deliver a tannin-like backbone to the blend. They decide to go for Johnny Rotten for practical reasons: the barrel is the top one of three stacked barrels, which will make it easier to move with a forklift. When driving the heavy barrels around the barrel and foeder hall nostalgia is put on hold.

To make the final decision on the right proportions both Koen and Alex make their own blend. Then they blind-taste it and the best one wins. Today it is Koen's blend that comes out best. Although I have to say 'best' to me sounds relative: I've noticed some subtle differences, but it's a close match. This tiny bit of competition shows Alex and Koen's camaraderie. And their tasting skills and dedication. 'We blend in a very intuitive way,' Alex says. 'Some breweries analyse the acidity of their beers and aim for a target acidity. We only use our noses and palates.'

Bringing tradition to a new audience is important for Alex and Koen, but they want to play with tradition too. In the case of Oud Bruin it has led them to infuse the aged beer with a variety of ingredients and then let it mature some more, picking up the aroma and flavour of the infused ingredient: strawberries, which we added today, or cherries, raspberries and grapes, but also more experimental additions like oak leaves.

Alex and Koen also play with the brewing and ageing techniques of Flanders browns either to dig a bit deeper into the history of the style or to produce some hybrid offspring. The brown ale that is the basis for Super Boil is boiled for 16 hours instead of the regular one and a half. Alex: 'I once read that brewers in 19th-century Oudenaarde used to do this, causing a maillard reaction which leads to caramelisation, a deeper brown colour and flavour because of more unfermentable sugars.' For Super Boil, which is brewed twice a year, 't Verzet organises an open 24-hour brewday in December.

Then there's Oaky Moaky, a stout that has aged in Ardbeg and Ardmore whisky barrels, which results in a complex aroma and flavour with a deep acidity, a well-rounded roasted character and a touch of smokiness. Or Kameradski Balsamico, a blend of an imperial stout with Oud Bruin that was left to age in barrels open to the air, in order to create balsamic-like acetic acid.

AN ACT OF RESISTANCE

While preparing my visit to 't Verzet I came across some website pictures of Alex and Koen wearing monkey masks. Today I've definitely got to know them as brewers who love to have fun throughout their brewdays. The play with rockstar names is one element of this. But what about the monkey masks?

'We started using them in 2016 when we launched a one-off beer named Scandinavian Pussy.' With the name of the beer Alex and Koen wanted to provoke Mikkel Borg Bjergsø of Danish beer brand Mikkeller for deridingly stating in an interview that you can train a monkey to brew a beer. Although they liked Mikkeller's beers they were upset by Bjergsø's apparent disrespect for the talent and hard work of brewers and decided to react with the language they know best: beer and brewing. Alex explains the name of the beer: 'He's a Scandinavian Pussy because he is too scared to run his own brewery.' (To this day the large majority of Mikkeller beers are produced through contract brewing, which is basically an arrangement between a beer company and a brewery to brew and package the beer company's recipe.) In the photo accompanying the release of the beer Alex and Koen wore monkey masks and they have been doing it ever since for beer releases.

Although brewing certainly is no monkey business, Alex and Koen sure can climb like monkeys. In order to check whether Joey Ramone is nearly filled with a new batch of brown ale I try to climb on top of the foeder. It's not without risk and I do it carefully. I stay there for a while until I give up my place to Alex, who is on top of the foeder in no time and seems pretty comfortable up there. Comfortable enough to keep a pleasant conversation going while the last bit of brown ale is flowing into the foeder.

And then, all of a sudden, Koen, who controls the pump, notices some beer leaking out of Joey's head. The pump is turned off quickly, but it can't prevent quite a lot of brown ale flowing from the foeder into a hard-to-reach corner of the hall. Talking about beer with a brewer is not without consequences. But I'm sure I'll be able to make it up in a minute. Some cleaning will have to be done, the part of the brewing process I'm beginning to excel at.

WORK-LIFE BALANCE

Alex would like to be home rather early today. He's got a date with his wife. 'Since we had children we go out on a date every month.' Alex and Koen share their private planners online, so they know when the other has planned something special and can't work late hours. Being passionate is essential for a craft brewer, but Alex and Koen also want to maintain a good work-life balance. A good balance — it's exactly what they want in their Oud Bruin as well.

It's time for me to go home too. It's my wife who's got a date. She's meeting up with some friends. When I get home it will be time to read a bedtime story and then tuck in the children. My companion for the night, while I type out the notes of the day, will be Kameradski Balsamico. And the date with my wife will be marked in our planner with vibrant colours. Time for some compensation for all the hours and days I set aside to write this book.

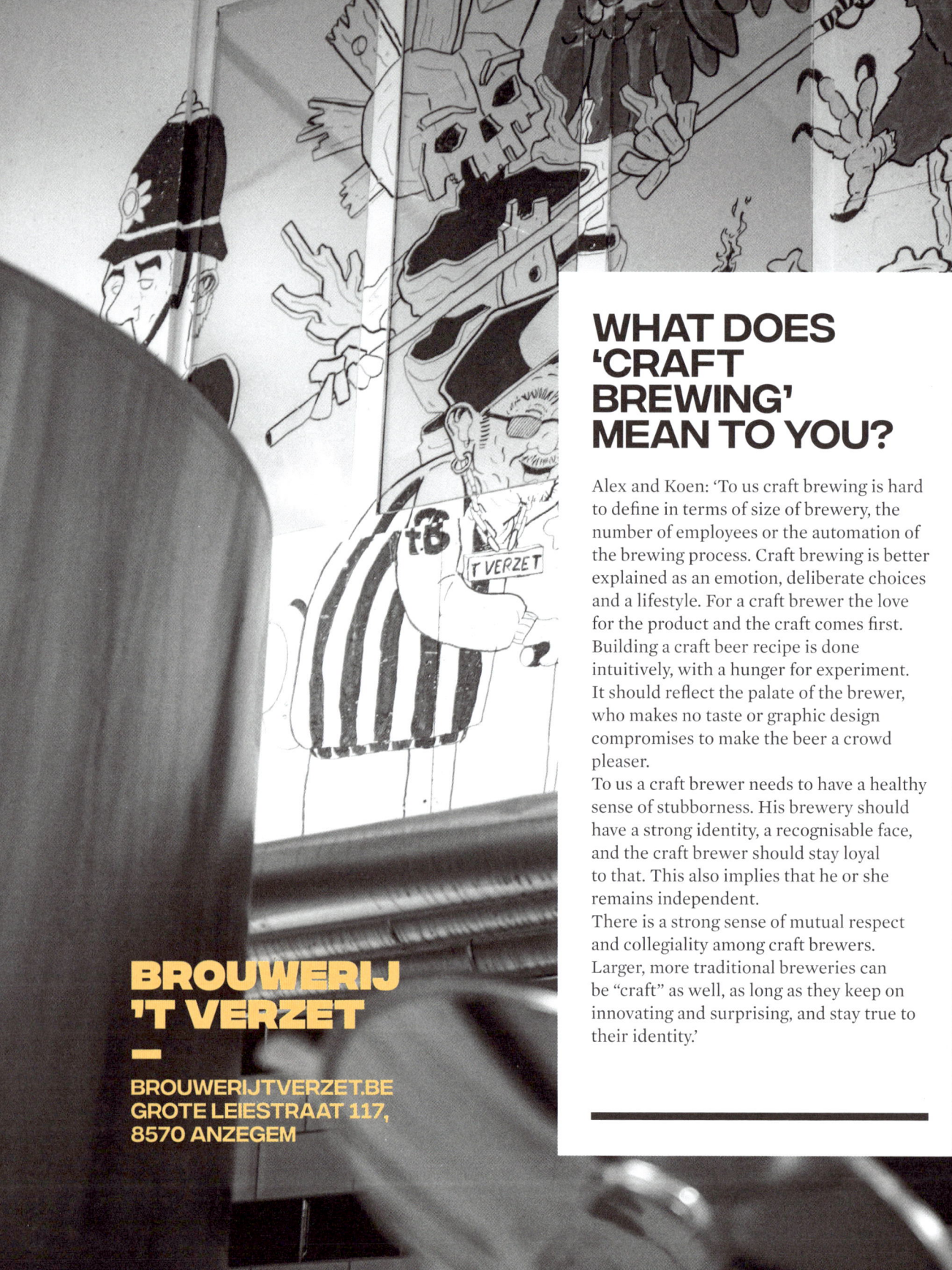

WHAT DOES 'CRAFT BREWING' MEAN TO YOU?

Alex and Koen: 'To us craft brewing is hard to define in terms of size of brewery, the number of employees or the automation of the brewing process. Craft brewing is better explained as an emotion, deliberate choices and a lifestyle. For a craft brewer the love for the product and the craft comes first. Building a craft beer recipe is done intuitively, with a hunger for experiment. It should reflect the palate of the brewer, who makes no taste or graphic design compromises to make the beer a crowd pleaser.

To us a craft brewer needs to have a healthy sense of stubborness. His brewery should have a strong identity, a recognisable face, and the craft brewer should stay loyal to that. This also implies that he or she remains independent.

There is a strong sense of mutual respect and collegiality among craft brewers. Larger, more traditional breweries can be "craft" as well, as long as they keep on innovating and surprising, and stay true to their identity.'

BROUWERIJ 'T VERZET
—
BROUWERIJTVERZET.BE
GROTE LEIESTRAAT 117,
8570 ANZEGEM

THE SIGNATURE BEERS OF 'T VERZET

SUPER NOAH
(4.9% ABV)

Super NoAH, which is an acronym for Super No American Hops, is a slightly hazy, straw-yellow session beer with a lacy head. The idea was to make a hoppy session ale with only Belgian hops, in order to show beer lovers that you don't need American hops to make pronounced light hoppy beers. In the nose Super NoAH is a bit floral with aromas of grass, pepper, herbs and some malt jumping to the front. It tastes very refreshing, with gentle citrus acidity as a first impression, some maltiness in the middle and a gentle bitterness in the finish, which makes for a light, well-balanced beer.

OUD BRUIN OAK LEAF
(6% ABV)

Oud Bruin Oak Leaf has hand-picked oak leaves added. They are covered with wild yeasts and add more complexity and acidity to Oud Bruin. It pours deep brown with a red glow and has the aroma of dried fruit tea with some green apple. A second impression is that of vanilla and beurre noisette. And after you let the beer breathe inside the glass for a bit the scent of forest comes to the surface. The flavour of Oud Bruin Oak Leaf is dominated by a fruity acidity that lingers for a while, steadily making room for subtle tannins.

KAMERADSKI BALSAMICO
(12.5% ABV)

This is one you will either love or hate, a maverick among beers. Not because of its strength — although you might consider 12.5% ABV a sledgehammer — but because of its unorthodox nature: a blend of an imperial stout with Oud Bruin, with a balsamic-like acidity. Kameradski Balsamico looks black with a ruby sparkle and a beige head. The aroma contains a strong sense of alcohol and a clear smell of balsamic, accentuated by notes of dried red fruits, some candy and coffee liqueur. A first sip gives away a syrupy mouthfeel. Kameradski Balsamico then comes in sweet and a tiny bit sour on the palate, with bitter hints of coffee and dark chocolate with currants. Complex and surprising from start to finish.

'Sombre melancholy of the Russian soul'

STOUT

Though porters and stouts today are usually quite expensive beers to make — with a complex and rich malt bill consisting of speciality malts — and a niche product in comparison to blond, hoppy beers, they (porters in particular) once were the people's beer, the world's first industrial ale.

From the craft brewers I met throughout my journey I gathered that stouts (and porters) are often their troubled pets, made with passion but not easy to bring to a larger audience. This hasn't prevented them and their colleagues worldwide from creating a huge variety of substyles with at least two things in common: porters and stouts are dark to pitch black and have a roasty character. The difference between a porter and a stout is as murky as their origins. To many beer connoisseurs they are substyles of one and the same category. This idea has a solid historical basis: the stout was originally a 'stout' porter or strong porter. Today 'stout' is the term used more often to refer to this type of beer.

Stouts inspire a lot of variation, as shown in this non-finite list: dry stout, milk stout, oatmeal stout, extra stout, coffee stout, chicory stout, oyster stout, chocolate stout, barrel-aged stout, sour stout, smoked stout and of course imperial stout. And let's not forget black IPA, which has the looks of a stout but doesn't taste like one (hardly), or golden stout, which doesn't look like a stout at all but more or less smells and tastes like one.

Stouts may not be bestsellers, but they certainly display a lot of creativity, and when beer geeks love a stout they really love it. Some stouts have gathered a huge following. Founders Breakfast Stout, for instance, or Left Hand Milk Stout, Old Rasputin Russian Imperial Stout and Black Albert, which was originally brewed by Belgian brewers De Struise Brouwers for the American Ebenezer's Pub and has plenty of fans on both sides of the Atlantic.

From murky to imperial

Porters and stouts come from humble beginnings in the early 18th century: a dark, murky ale for London's working classes, many working as porters. With the help of new industrial malting techniques, a growing knowledge of the brewing process and an enhanced use of hops — conditions that also stimulated the emergence of pale ales — porters and stouts became better, hoppier, more complex, stronger, and were made with higher industrial efficiency for a democratic price. From a drink for porters it became a valued export product, popular in the Baltic region and Russia, and even at the Russian imperial court (hence imperial stout). The interest in stouts nearly collapsed in the last decades of the 20th century, most notably in the country of origin, England. But worldwide interest was revived via the writings of Michael Jackson and American craft beer pioneers like (again) Anchor Brewing in the 1970s. Closer to the 'birth place' of porters and stouts CAMRA (Campaign for Real Ale) played a vital part in their revival 1990s and early 2000s.

Today stouts are as imperial as they once were, par excellence being a beer to taste slowly, taking your time on the sofa, as you would for a single malt whisky. Especially on a cold winter's night when a strong stout can warm your heart and make your thoughts deep. Like German beer writer Horst Dornbusch said: 'an imperial stout is a metaphor for the sombre melancholy of the Russian soul.' Now I know where that feeling comes from: during those winter nights I must feel a bit Russian.

Imperial coffee stout

For this beer I set the bar high, because my quest for a better understanding of brewing had started with a failed imperial stout, one of my favourite beer styles. This imperial coffee stout was also a challenging beer to brew at home, with a grist of more than 4 kilos for a 20 litre kettle. It was barely large enough.

FOR 11 LITRES STOUT

MALT: *3.3 kg of pilsner malt, 300 g of Special B, 300 g of Munich, 150 g of wheat, 150 g of chocolate malt, 150 g of black malt, 150 g of flaked oats*
HOP: *10 g of Brewer's Gold, 10 g of East Kent Goldings, 10 g of El Dorado*
YEAST: *SafAle S-04*
EXTRA: *Irish moss, 500 g of candi sugar*

MASH

— Add 16.5 litres of water to a kettle and attach the brewbag to the handles of the kettle. Warm up the water to 68°C.

75' —— Pour in the milled malts. The water will drop in temperature to about 67°C.
Hold at 67°C for 60 minutes. Gently keep on stirring the malts.

70' —— Adjust pH to 5.4.

15' —— Heat up to 78°C to end enzyme activity.

— Pull out the bag, let it drain (don't squeeze it). You should be able to start the boil with 15 litres of wort with a pre-boil original gravity of 1068.

BOIL

70' —— Start to boil the wort. Just before it starts boiling adjust pH to 5.2.

60' —— Boil for 60 minutes. Add Brewer's Gold (10 g).

35' —— Add East Kent Goldings (10 g).

10' —— Add Irish moss and 500 g of candi sugar.

00' —— Add El Dorado (10 g).

FERMENTATION

- Cool down the wort to 25°C.
- Measure the specific gravity of the wort. You should reach an original gravity of 1090.
- Transfer to the fermentation bucket. Sprinkle the dry yeast over the wort.
- Let it ferment for a week at 20–22°C. Final gravity should be around 1020, approximately 9% ABV.

LAGERING AND DRY-HOPPING

- Transfer the beer to the lagering bucket. Don't transfer the sediment.
- Add 90 g of coarsely ground coffee in a hop bag and let it lager for another week in a cooler place.

BOTTLING AND BOTTLE CONDITIONING

- Boil 70 g of sugar (7 g per litre) in a small amount of water. Let it cool down to 25°C.
- Remove the bags with the coffee from the bucket and add the sugar water. Gently stir it with a sanitised spoon. Close the lid. You're ready to start bottling.
- Put the bottles in a warm dark place. Imperial stouts, or any high-gravity beers such as barley wines, need more time to carbonate. Instead of a week you should keep the bottles warm for three to four weeks. These types of beer get better with time.

BREWING NOTES

- Impatiently looking forward to taste the final result, I opened a bottle after one week of bottle conditioning. Too soon. Like brewing theory predicts, the beer was flat. It wasn't until after three weeks that it had become fizzy, and for the nice beige frothy head you would expect from an imperial coffee stout I had to wait 5 weeks.
- Be careful with those coffee beans. The first time I brewed this recipe I added 90 g and let it rest for a week. The coffee aroma and flavour were a bit too strong. For a next batch I only added 50 g, which was sufficient for the subtle touch of coffee I wanted.

'BUSINESS IN THE FRONT, PARTY IN THE BACK'

BRASSERIE DU BORINAGE

Festival de la coupe mulet

Antoine Malingret and Damien Hubert have big plans this weekend. In Boussu, close to Mons, they are organising the first European *Festival de la coupe mulet*, or the 'mullet haircut festival'. I knew that trying to meet them this week would be difficult.

When I arrive at Brasserie du Borinage, formerly Ça brasse pour moi, I see people being busily moving from the brewery to a van and back, carrying parts of a tap installation. I should recognise Antoine and Damien from their many Facebook posts. Neither of them is here. Then I notice another van... No, not Antoine or Damien either.

My phone is ringing. It's Damien. 'Sorry we're not there yet, Jeroen, we've got a bit of an emergency situation here, but we'll be there right away. Make yourself comfortable in the meantime.'

I contacted Brasserie du Borinage to join a brewday, but because of the festival they couldn't fit one into their schedule. I suggested I could lend a hand with some heavy labour to prepare the festival site and get to know the whole beer festival thing from the inside.

Nele has arrived too. We stroll around the brewery site awaiting Antoine and Damien. I can see quite a lot of work needs to be done. They've been moving things around and somehow stopped midway. It's quiet here. Too quiet. The calm before the storm. But hey, they've got two more days until D-Day.

Then Antoine and Damien arrive, in a black van, A-Team style, obviously in a hurry but still keeping their cool. This impression gets a boost from their appearance: *coupe mulet*, a mullet haircut, also known as a Kentucky waterfall, and a bristly moustache. 'It's not just dressing up for the festival,' Damien will later tell me, although the occasion plays a part in it.

DÉWANNE

'I have to admit, we don't have much time. There's so much we need to do,' Damien says. Antoine looks contemplative. Behind the moustache there's worry on his face. 'I came here to help wherever I can,' I tell them. For these brewers' stories I always want some brewery action. This may not be a brewday, but I sense it's going to be a really active one, doing things with these guys that are an integral part of running a craft brewery that wants to reach out to beer lovers and the local community.

'Well, there is something you can help us with,' Damien says slightly hesitantly. 'We need to make a delivery to a hotel bar in Brussels...' I know where he is heading. 'Sure, I can do that — to go back home I need to drive past Brussels anyway.' They both seem delighted. 'You should take ten kegs there,' Antoine tells me. 'I have to carbonate them and then they're ready to go.'

'If you want to, we can unload the van in the meantime and then I'll show you around and tell you about our plans for this weekend,' Damien says. 'Antoine, can we show them how you carbonate the kegs?' he asks. 'Well, I'd rather you didn't. I need to focus. Nothing can go wrong. We don't want to sell kegs with bad carbonation.'

No problem, Antoine, whatever it takes for good, well-carbonated beer.

Damien opens the back of the van. It's loaded with flight cases and microphone stands, for the gigs on Saturday. We put the stuff in an old shipping container. When we're done Damien takes us up to the roof of the container. 'Here we'll have a hair salon. We want visitors who haven't got a mullet yet to have one cut. It's going to be fun.'

From the container roof we have a good view over the festival site. 'The festival will be on the premises of the brewery and on this patch of grassland behind it. It's town property. The town is really supportive of the festival and gave us permission to use the patch and tear down the wall separating it from the brewery. We only tore it down yesterday. Yeah, it's all pretty last minute,' Damien says, confirming my initial impression.

Back down on the ground, Damien tells us the mullet haircut is a lot like the brewery's philosophy: 'Business in the front, party in the back. Like the seriousness of short hair in the front we are serious about our business, about our beers and the craft to make them. But we're trying to make a lot of fun as well and do all sorts of crazy, over-the-top stuff. In our local dialect — the word does not exist in standard French — we call that "*déwanne*". The long hair at the back is *déwanne*.'

And so is this festival and the work that needs to be done to get ready for... 'More than 3000 people if everyone shows up who said so on the Facebook event page. In any case we are allowed to let 3000 people in. We never thought we would get even near that number.'

BOUSSU, BORINAGE, BELGIUM

'Brasserie du Borinage is about more than brewing and selling beer. We are part of this local community. We were born and raised here in the Borinage, a region with a lot of unemployment and bad economic prospects. We want to show that we can do business here and do it our way,' Damien tells us while we're heading towards the other side of the terrain. His words are emphasised by the contrast between the playground of the local primary school on one side — the future of this town — and on the other the derelict building with a gate that will be the entrance on Saturday — a symbol of the past of this troubled region.

'We don't know of any business, company or firm in the Borinage that uses "Borinage" as part of its name. We do on purpose. People here have very low self-esteem and we want to do something about this. Make *Borains* proud of the Borinage.' And humour — self-mockery and irony — plays an important role in that, as shown in beers like Boriner Vice, with a label showing a man's feet wearing green plastic sandals and white sports socks, or Urine, a double IPA and festival special mocking the piss-like beers many music festivals serve.

The festival itself seems to me like the summit of this regained pride/self-mockery alliance. When I visit it on Saturday I witness a lively, cordial atmosphere, people of all ages having fun. Some look like they have really time-travelled from the 1980s, others are their everyday selves and are here just for fun and good beer, while most visitors are somewhere in between, having interpreted the festival as a huge fancy-dress party, wearing mullet wigs and wacky sunglasses. It doesn't matter, the fun and *la déwanne* prevail.

And still, at the festival there's also business in the front. When I arrive, local TV is doing an interview with Damien. The festival received a lot of buzz and seems to be very welcomed in the region. Damien and Antoine know what they are doing. On Wednesday you would have thought they were improvising; on Saturday you could see they've really pulled it off.

RTBF, RTL, *Le Soir*, *Paris Match*, Vice. Both national and (some) international press paid quite a bit of attention to the *Festival de la coupe mulet*. It isn't a coincidence. The press release shows the festival was well prepared and the idea behind it well articulated. And in Europe there is nothing like it.

FUNNY NAMES, SERIOUS CONTENT

The vision behind the festival is reflected in some choices Antoine and Damien make. L'Empire, one of their signature beers, is only served at the main bar, a means to monitor consumption and keep it under control. This imperial lager of 10% ABV is a heavy one, but easy to drink and thirst-quenching. A bad combination at a festival, trouble guaranteed. And trouble, if as an outsider I've understood it correctly, is not *déwanne*.

For the festival Brasserie du Borinage released two new beers: Kentucky Waterfalls, a pils, and Urine, a double IPA. Funny names, yes, but the content, like all beers of Brasserie du Borinage, is serious and a lot closer to the source of the ingredients than one would expect.

The brewery is housed inside the old farm buildings of Antoine's grandparents, and his father is still an active farmer, with fields down the road from the brewery. 'My father grows five grain varieties: wheat, rye, oat, spelt, and barley of course', Antoine explains. 'The first four varieties we use in the brewing process in their unmalted form, while the barley is malted at the Malterie du Château in Beloeil, 15 kilometres away. It enters the TerraBrew network, which connects farmers, malters and brewers.'

'All our beers contain some raw grains from the farm.' The beers may be inspired by international trends, have funny names, be playful and *déwanne*, but they are also rooted in a long regional and family tradition.

At the same time, Antoine and Damien are trying to be innovative in the way they sell craft beer. Alongside more classical distribution, they offer people the opportunity to appreciate their beers on the brewery site, at the Festival de la coupe mulet, for instance, the Apéro du dimanche, and food pairing and beer tasting events. Antoine and Damien also travel with their 'Déwanne mobile', a vintage caravan turned into a crazy beer truck, and they collaborate with local chefs and restaurants to enhance the link between craft beer and gastronomy. In general, Antoine and Damien consider their commercial relationships as true partnerships, going both ways.

Antoine and Damien also value an opportunity to promote their beers outside their home region, like the one presented by the hotel where I'll make a delivery in about an hour and a half. All ten kegs are carbonated and we can load them inside my car. I'm a bit wary about the weight of these kegs, especially because Antoine tells me I will also have to transport the tap installation and a large bottle of CO_2 — I don't drive a van! But if I drive carefully I should be able to make it without damaging my car's suspension.

Back at home, after a successful drop-off, I watch the video clip for L'Empire. Shot in the best French movie tradition, including the baritone voiceover, it tells the story of a group of soldiers from Napoleon's army that get lost *au mitan du Borinage*, in the middle of the Borinage. One after the other succumbs to exhaustion and thirst, until the last one, the leader on a horse — *une jument* or mare to be precise — sees a bottle of L'Empire and whispers with his last powers: '*Ma jument pour une Empire*', 'My mare for an Empire'. It turns out this is only a story told for the umpteenth time by one of the regulars at the counter of a local bar, somewhere in the heart of the Borinage, *au mitan des terrils*, surrounded by the many mining spoil heaps that define the image of the region. The place that also defines Brasserie du Borinage.

Although I don't understand a single word of the *patois* the characters and even the voiceover speak, I can see it's witty, creative, full of cultural references, and playing with the reputation of the Borinage and Boriner pub life in particular. But it's also a professionally made video, with an interesting narrative and shot with cinematographic skills. This isn't a gimmick, but creative work by some men with plans, who embrace social media as much as they embrace the mash rake. For Brasserie du Borinage it is business in the front and party in the back.

BRASSERIE DU BORINAGE

—

BRASSERIEDUBORINAGE.BE
RUE DU CALVAIRE 21,
7300 BOUSSU

WHAT DOES 'CRAFT BREWING' MEAN TO YOU?

Damien and Antoine: 'Craft brewing to us is dealing with modernity, allowing no (or very few) limits to creativity, making absolutely zero concessions to the market or to common taste. Like a chef, a craft brewer is an uninhibited magician mixing various ingredients to create the ultimate beer: a beer with a strong personality and a sharp style that dares and claims to be different.'

THE SIGNATURE BEERS OF BRASSERIE DU BORINAGE

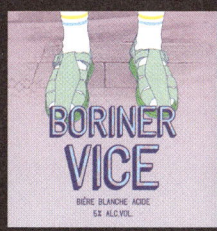

BORINER VICE
(5% ABV)

The name of this Berliner weisse is a pun on Miami Vice, on the reputation of the Borinage being a backward region, showcasing bad sartorial taste (also a satirical element on the label), and of course on Berliner weisse. It is a kettle soured wheat beer with some versatile characteristics.

The first impression in the nose is one of tropical fruit, with chardonnay notes. You would expect it's rather sweet too. On the palate, however, lacto acids are prominent from the start. They slowly give room to more bitter notes, which set the tone in the finish. Appearances — aromas in this case — can be deceptive.

RAYON DE SOLEIL
(6.2% ABV)

This rye saison is a blend of a young saison with a barrel-aged one 'infected' with Brettanomyces. The unmalted rye was grown and harvested by Antoine and Damien on Antoine's parental farm.

The aroma contains green apple, some cider character and has some brett just below the surface, waiting to become more prominent in due course. The earthy brett notes are also there on the palate, forming a nice threesome with hop bitterness and subtle malty sweetness.

L'EMPIRE
(10% ABV)

L'Empire is an imperial lager, an exceptionally strong blond fermented with lager yeast. The malt bill consists of pilsen, wheat and spelt — the unmalted wheat and spelt again coming from the Malingret farm. With a sweet malt character upfront you can expect a sturdy beer from the first aroma impression, although some similarities with lighter lagers and pilsners are there too: the herbal hop notes, for instance, and the absence of yeast elements like esters and phenols. Tasting it confirms this impression: it's malty, well carbonated and has a gentle hop-bitter finish. Like lagers do. But then a lot stronger. This is a pilsner on steroids. One that is dangerously easy to drink.

The Germans are back

GOSE

Ever since the early days craft brewing has been much about reviving beer styles that were pushed into oblivion by the big industry lagers. First the 19th-century English styles were reinterpreted, then American craft brewers made Belgian-style beers instead of importing them, and more recently German beer styles, sour ones in particular, are inspiring craft brewers and homebrewers worldwide to discover new territory.

The German beer styles of old are, among other things, appreciated for their yeast-driven character. The hefeweizen is characterised by the large amount of wheat malt used, up to 50%, and an ester-rich aroma and flavour with banana and clove notes. Kölsch is a hybrid ale-lager, top-fermented and cold-lagered, giving it a distinctive character for a beer low in alcohol.

The gose and Berliner weisse are also sessionable wheat beers, but historically they are closer to Belgian lambics, spontaneously fermented sour ales. Today a gose and a Berliner weisse get their sour character from kettle souring, a technique to sour the pre-boiled wort with Lactobacillus in 24–48 hours, instead of the extensive ageing process of traditional sour ales.

Surprising combinations

Given that craft brewers are looking for different flavours all the time and trying to push the boundaries, sometimes by embracing extreme or unexpected flavours, kettle souring is growing in popularity, as are the German sour beer styles, with lots of flavour but not too much alcohol (between 3 and 5% ABV).

Because of their acidity these are beers that combine well with fruit additions. The Berliner weisse originally used to be sweetened with a fruit syrup, an unattractive idea for most beer lovers, but one that inspired Florida-based brewers to experiment with all sorts of sweet tropical fruits native to the Sunshine State. Today they call it the Florida weisse.

The salty and sour character of a gose in its turn has also led to some interesting interpretations, one being the chocolate gose, which brings together sweet, sour, salty and bitter taste elements. On top of the addition of salt to the boil, typical for the style, cocoa nibs are added post-fermentation.

Kettle souring is also used to make hoppy sour ales. Traditional sours can't be hoppy, for two reasons. The aromas and flavours of the hops will have disappeared by the time the beer is ready to drink. And fresh hops stop Lactobacillus and Pediococcus, keeping the beer from turning sour quick enough to preserve it. A kettle soured beer on the other hand is already sour before the different stages of hop additions occur, in the boil or particularly in secondary fermentation, when a beer can be dry-hopped.

Kettle soured strawberry spelt gose

Kettle soured beers are well suited to brewing on a hot summer's day, because Lactobacillus needs higher temperatures to thrive, the recommended temperature range even being 40–46°C. But because for a homebrewer that's hard to maintain for 24–48 hours (you don't have time to babysit your beer) I've used a strain in this recipe that works well at (higher) room temperature.

Spelt is an ancient wheat variety, with similar characteristics to wheat, but also some interesting differences, like giving the beer a spicy touch, something that may suit this beer well.

FOR 11 LITRES SPELTGOSE

MALT: *1.3 kg of pilsner malt, 650 g of wheat malt, 650 g of spelt malt*
HOP: *5 g of Goldings*
YEAST: *WYEAST 5335 (Lactobacillus blend), WYEAST 1007 (German ale yeast)*
EXTRA: *Irish moss, 7 g of sea salt, 14 g of dried coriander seeds, 1 kg of frozen strawberries*

MASH

— Add 16 litres of water to a kettle and attach the brewbag to the handles of the kettle. Warm up the water to 65°C.

80' — Pour in the milled malts. The water will drop in temperature to about 64°C.
Hold at 64°C for 60 minutes. Gently keep on stirring the malts.

70' — Adjust pH to 5.4.

20' — Heat up to 78°C.

— Pull out the bag, let it drain. You should be able to start the boil with 15 litres of wort with a pre-boil original gravity of 1040.

BOIL 1

— Boil for 5 minutes. Cool down to 45°C and transfer into a kettle you can seal off completely. A glass fermentation bottle or demijohn might work too.
— Lower pH to 4.5 with refined lactic acid and then add the contents of the smackpack of WYEAST 5335 to the wort. Gently stir. Let it sit for 24–48 hours, depending on the level of acidity you like. Take a sample every 12 hours to check the pH: a pH around 3.5 is common for a gose. Or you can taste the acidity, but don't swallow: at this pre-boil stage the wort may still contain some pathogens.

BOIL 2

100' —— Start to boil the wort (be aware that the smell of soured wort being boiled may be awful, but it doesn't mean you've spoiled the beer)

90' —— Boil for 90 minutes.

60' —— Add Goldings (5 g).

10' —— Add Irish moss (5 g), sea salt (7 g) and coriander seeds (14 g).

00' —— Stop the boil.

FERMENTATION

— Cool down the wort to 25°C.
— Measure the specific gravity of the wort. You should reach an original gravity of 1055.
— Transfer to the fermentation bucket and add the yeast. Give it a stir with a sanitised spoon.
— Let it ferment for a week at around 20°C. Final gravity should be 1015, approximately 5.2% ABV.

LAGERING AND FRUIT ADDITION

— Transfer the beer to the lagering bucket. Don't transfer the sediment.
— Add the frozen strawberries.
— Let it lager for one to two weeks in a cooler place. Then siphon the beer to another lagering bucket and let it sit for about a month before bottling.

BOTTLING AND BOTTLE CONDITIONING

— Boil 70 g of sugar (7 g per litre) in a small amount of water. Let it cool down to 25°C and add the sugar water. Gently stir it with a sanitised spoon and close the lid. You're ready to start bottling.
— Put the bottles in a warm dark place for a week in order to carbonate the beer. Then let it rest for another week in a cooler place or a fridge.

BREWING NOTE

— For the addition of the strawberries you've got a couple of options, depending on how much strawberry you want in your beer:
  - For a subtle strawberry flavour and hardly any colouring, put them in a hop bag.
  - Most likely you will want both a pronounced strawberry flavour and a nice pink beer. Lightly squash the strawberries and add them to the beer, giving them a slight stir.
  - If you want to do it the Florida weisse way, mash the strawberries with a potato masher and stir them well through the beer. When bottling, don't siphon the beer into another bucket, but bottle straight from the lagering bucket with the mashed strawberries. Bottling will be slower, but you'll enhance the smoothie effect in your beer.

'A CRAFT BREWER SHOULD BREW TO ASTONISH PEOPLE'

ATRIUM BRASSERIE ARTISANALE

The One — saison

One wouldn't expect a cosmopolitan brewpub in the centre of Marche-en-Famenne, a town in the heart of the Belgian Ardennes, known to many Belgians for the untimely death in 1934 of the Belgian king Albert I. In fact, this popular king fell from a rock in... a different Marche, Marche-les-Dames, near Namur. Just to say that this beautiful but discrete town of about 17,000 inhabitants doesn't spontaneously bring many cultural references or postcard images to the mind of the non-*Marchwis*.

In terms of beer culture I have always associated it with very traditional Wallonian beers and the fact that it's not too far from Rochefort. At least, that was until the end of 2018, when Paula Yunes and Valéry De Breucker opened Atrium brasserie artisanale, a brewery with a taproom, in the town centre, in Rue des Brasseurs or Brewers' Street.

'It was a huge change for us, coming from São Paulo in Brazil with its 20 million inhabitants. But we immediately knew this was the place. A building we could shape to our needs, right in front of a hotel. And in Rue des Brasseurs! The conditions were perfect,' Valéry says.

It turned out the locals were also happy to have a new brewery and taproom in town. 'The hotel serves our beers in its bar and restaurant, and they're even available in the minibar.' I get the impression the warm, inviting attitude of Valéry has something to do with the smooth interaction between Atrium and its neighbour entrepreneurs. Before we start talking about beer Valéry takes Nele and me to the baker's around the corner, to get some croissants — brewing is better started on a full stomach, because you never know when the process will allow the next meal. By the convivial way the bakery shop assistant addresses Valéry one would assume he buys croissants every day.

DELICATE DRIVING

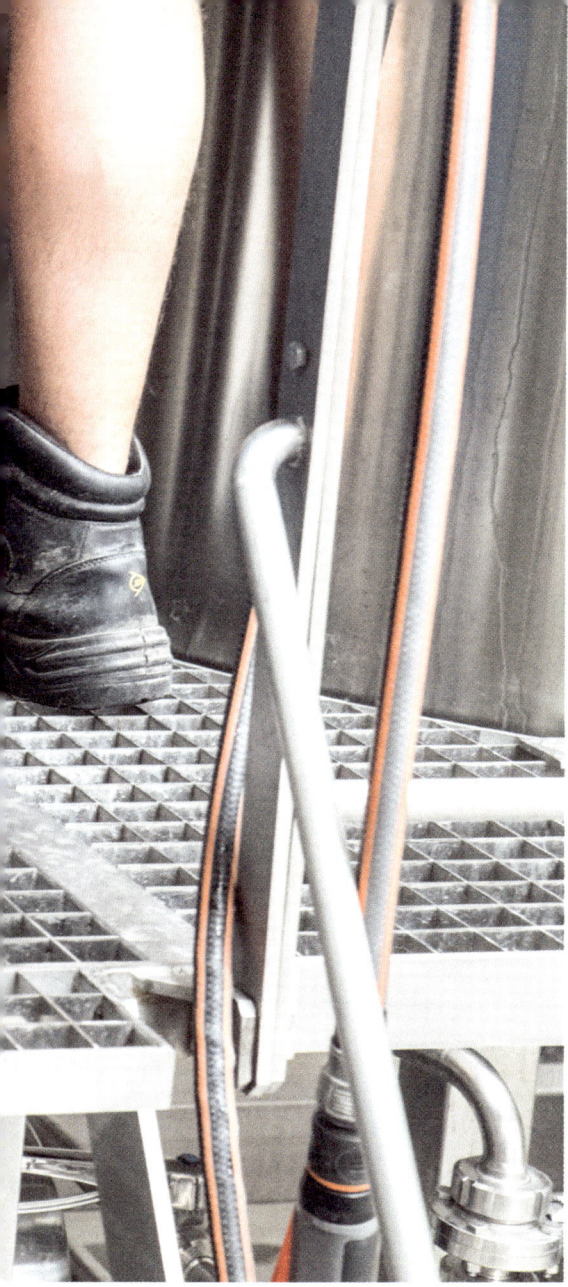

'The One is our interpretation of a saison, with a lot of wheat, some coriander and the saison yeast strain we culture ourselves. It was the first beer Valéry and I brewed together in Brazil and the first one we brewed when we opened the brewery. We also brewed it for our wedding. That's why we called it The One,' Paula tells me while we're enjoying a croissant and a glass of orange juice. She arrived a couple of minutes ago and turns out to be as open and inviting as Valéry.

'The One is also the most popular beer in the taproom.' Valéry tells me it serves as a bridge to bring the more traditional locals to the other, American-inspired and cosmopolitan Atrium beers. 'We also want to use it as a platform for a range of occasional variations that we would call The 1.2 or The 1.3 and so on. We recently did 20 litres flavoured with camomile and one with rosehip,' Paula adds. 'The rosehip saison came out a beautiful pink.'

Strengthened by the calorie-rich croissants, it's time to start brewing. The water has reached strike temperature and the grains have been milled. Valéry drives a lift truck with a container full of grist to the mash tun. The forklift and some delicate driving take the container right above the pipe that leads into the mash tun. It's a precision job Valéry clearly masters, a craft in its own right. 'Hangovers on a brewday are not an option,' he shouts from the truck.

In the pipe the grains are mixed with water at the right strike temperature and then poured into the mash tun, to avoid oxidation of the grains. Valéry has already filled the bottom of the lauter tun with rice husks, to better filter the mash. 'With a grain bill like this, with up to 20% wheat malt, filtering is difficult. The rice husks should help to make a nice filter bed. Because it's only the husks we use, it won't influence the flavour or aroma.'

The plan was to brew Clémentine, a wheat beer with clementines, but the special yeast hasn't arrived in time from the US. Paula and Valéry want this yeast strain because it smooths the acidity typical for a Belgian white. Today they will brew an extra batch of their bestselling beer The One instead.

YES, WE CAN

On Paula and Valéry's first brewday here the brewhouse's computer program still needed to be fine-tuned. Instead of the desired temperature rest of 62°C the temperature inside the mash tun was 74°C, so the crucial step in which the beta-amylase enzyme converts starch into fermentable sugars was skipped. No fermentable sugars means no alcohol means no beer. Paula and Valéry had to flush their very first 1000 litres down the drain.

Today the temperature is perfect. A nice 62°C. One hour to go.

'While mashing is ongoing Paula and I need to do some measurements in the front of the taproom,' Valéry tells me. 'We're getting a Luxembourg company with a mobile canning machine to come over to try one of our beers in cans. We'll start with 1000 litres to see the response from the local community.'

Here in Marche-en-Famenne they know a thing or two about beers. The region is rich in traditional Belgian beers, with three Trappist breweries close by. 'But people here need some time to discover and appreciate the new styles and tastes. It's one of the reasons we are not canning beer yet. If people hear about beer in cans Cara Pils is what comes to mind.' Cara Pils is the economy house beer of a Belgian supermarket chain. It's cheap and it's sold in cans. For many Belgian beer consumers one plus one is two. And in this case the maths doesn't work.

Paula and Valéry do it all together: brewing, paperwork, bartending in the taproom... and welcoming an inquisitive beer writer.

'Cans are better for the quality and shelf life of the beer, because absolutely no light can reach the beer and it's completely sealed off from oxygen,' Paula says with fire. 'On top of that, in contrast to what many people think, it is more ecological. Cans are 100% reusable and come with a lower financial and ecological cost to recycle than bottles.' And cans are a great canvas for artistic beer labels.

With brewing workshops, zythology classes, tastings and concerts Paula and Valéry reach out to the local community. It's important to them, even though, or maybe precisely because, they aren't from the region. Valéry grew up in Anderlecht and started travelling the world after he got fed up with his first job. He had been globetrotting for 12 years, spending quite some time in Australia, before he moved to Brazil in 2011. That's where he met Paula.

Paula, a São Paulo local, worked for a beer importer who specialised in American, Belgian and Japanese beers. 'She interviewed me when I applied for a job,' Valéry recalls. Once colleagues, they hit it off with each other and soon became a couple.

Paula has been in the Brazilian beer business for quite a long time. She started an online beer shop with a friend, worked as a brand manager for a medium-sized Brazilian brewery and is a certified zythologist. She was also a TV host for a local homebrew reality show called *Cervejantes*, a Portuguese neologism you can translate as 'beer people'. It was a slightly over the top, tongue in cheek kind of show, every episode showcasing a beer contest between two homebrewers who have to brew the better version of a beer, starting from the same given theme and style.

BURNOUT DANGER

From the fun part of beer and brewing to the serious stuff. A man knocks at the door. He is in his fifties and wears unfashionable glasses. He looks like he reads spreadsheets at breakfast and takes calculators to bed. 'Sorry, Jeroen, that's the excise duty inspector,' Valéry apologises. 'He's here to collect some samples of previous batches. It'll only take a minute.'

'Trouble?' I ask Valéry when the inspector has left. 'No. Business as usual. We heard so many stories about excise duty inspectors, but we actually have been lucky. We wanted to be ready to start brewing early November 2018, so we could launch our beers when everybody was looking for the perfect Christmas or New Year's gift. But we didn't have our permit yet. A clerk at the excise duty office was really understanding and made sure we got the permit in time. If we'd missed that opportunity, it might have given us a tricky start.'

But that was not the case. Things are moving well now, and Paula and Valéry have got their hands full. Too full, perhaps. 'We had a bit of a burnout a couple of weeks ago. We were doing everything, just the two of us. Brewing, the taproom, the visuals, the administration. And we live right next door, so we always see things that need doing. It was a bit too much. Coincidentally the local Chamber of Commerce held a lecture for start-up businesses in the region about keeping a good work-life balance. It was the perfect timing for us. Since then we have decided not to open the taproom on Thursdays any more.' And recently they've taken on an employee too.

The idea to start their own brewery emerged pretty soon after they met. But the road towards that goal wasn't always easy. 'When we came back to Belgium we started brewing classes. I worked at Fantôme brewery in Soy, but Paula didn't have a job and we were sometimes short of money. To make an extra living we were brewing beers on demand at people's homes. It was a nice way to experiment and perfect our brewing skills.'

Brewing beers on demand would be economically sensible in order to make the brewery more profitable. 'We get a lot of requests from homebrewers to brew their homebrew recipes, but we don't want to do that. We want to brew our own beers,' Paula says. 'The only exception we make are friends and collabs. We'll probably brew the beer of some friends from Brazil, Cervejaria Dádiva. We would love to introduce them to Belgian and European beer lovers and it will be cheaper and more ecological to brew their beers here than to import them. So it would be a win-win situation.

'We recently also did a collab with Brasserie de la Sambre. The result is Sombra, a black IPA that we'll present at Zythos Beer Festival in April. Sombra has got the signature of both breweries. We love a malty backbone in our beers and Brasserie de la Sambre is for hop-forward beers. A black IPA is like a good marriage of both.'

Atrium attended Zythos, Belgium's largest beer festival, for the first time in 2019 and made quite an impression. Beer lovers at the festival named them second best brewery on the Brewer Stage app, and both Onyx and Onyx Amburana made it to the top 10 of best beers.

135

LE STOUT

Today the taproom is closed, but the gates are rolled open and now and then a regular customer peeps in. Jacques, a Friday regular who loves Onyx, the Atrium stout, stops by while we're having a taste of a previous batch of The One, straight from the fermenter. He happily takes a sip too. Some yeast is still in suspension, which makes it quite fruity. Malt flavours are very present too. Although it's never easy to tell what the final result, the beer you pour from the bottle, will taste like from a sample straight from the fermenter, this sample of The One resembles a maltier blond with a pronounced wheat character.

These non-typical saison characteristics — whatever that means with a beer style as versatile as the brewer's brewing mood and the ingredients available — come back in the bottle we open at lunchtime. This is definitely an all-grain beer, with 6.5% ABV and a full body, which displays spicy and yeasty notes, but is a little less dry than some of the commonly known saisons.

'Saisons can come in all shapes and sizes. However, we always aim for 6.5% ABV. But I have to admit that The One we brewed for our wedding was a lot stronger, about 10% ABV. Quite a few relatives got really drunk that night,' Valéry says with a smile.

Jacques likes the beer too. But to him there is nothing like Onyx. 'The Atrium stout is extraordinary, something fantastic. Every Friday I drink one. Or two, but that's a bit dangerous, because it's very strong.'

Now that local customers are getting to know the core beers of Atrium, they are developing certain preferences, like Jacques. Paula and Valéry want to help them discover what they like or don't like in beer. Given there is so much variety, even within the range of nine beers, there's one for everybody's palate. 'But when women ask for women's beer, I don't like that question. And it's asked a lot,' Paula says. 'I don't understand it. Men and women eat the same food, drink the same wine, but when it comes to beer all of a sudden people think of it in separate categories.' Paula seems to me the perfect person to advocate against that stereotype, starting here in Marche-en-Famenne.

COSMOPOLITAN APPROACH

While Paula and I have been talking to Jacques, Valéry has finished the lautering process. It's about time to collect the spent grains from the lautering tun. But first Paula shows me the clementines that will flavour Clémentine. Paula and Valéry only use the clementine zest, without the pith, to avoid any sharp bitterness.

I tried Clémentine at home before I visited Atrium and found the clementine notes very subtle. At no point do you really taste the fruit, but the infusion gives a nice complexity to the beer, which has characteristics of both a Belgian wheat beer and a German hefeweizen.

Emptying the lautering tun goes easily. The rake does most of the work and gives us plenty of time to talk. About brewing, mostly — that's what I'm here for in the first place. And about living in Belgium, getting used to life here, about the somehow huge differences between Belgium and Brazil. Both good — Belgium and Marche-en-Famenne in particular are a lot safer than São Paulo — and bad — life's less sunny in Belgium, in a figurative and a literal sense. The first winter, Paula was always cold, even inside the house. Valéry remembers how she always raised the thermostat to the point that he couldn't bear the heat any more.

Valéry drives a lift truck with a container full of grist to the mash tun. A precision job, as you can see. 'Hangovers on a brewday are not an option.'

Bringing Brazilian tropical conditions to the Ardennes wasn't possible, but Paula and Valéry have brought a touch of Brazil to Marche-en-Famenne in other ways. The decoration of the taproom and the furniture refer to the Brazilian *boteco*, a people's bar that serves alcoholic beverages and snacks. Carya, a brown ale much like a Belgian dubbel, is given an American twist by adding pecan nuts. And then there are the beers aged in barrels made of indigenous Brazilian wood like amburana and balsam.

To keep the barrels moist they were transported containing a tiny bit of cachaça, a Brazilian spirit. No need to declare it at customs, as by the time it got here the cachaça had evaporated. But the wood still gives off plenty of flavours from the spirit. One of the barrels, made of amburana, is filled with Onyx. This way, an already complex imperial stout ages into an even more complex beer.

The wort for The One has been boiled by now and while it is being transferred to the fermentation tank we round off this brewday with a late lunch: some sandwiches from the bakery around the corner. So, Valéry doesn't only buy croissants there after all.

Instead of a cup of coffee we finish lunch with two tasting glasses of Onyx, one from a bottle and one from the amburana barrel. What I get to taste from the barrel still needs some blending with an unbarrelled Onyx, but the amburana certainly gives an interesting aroma of cinnamon, something that is new to the whole palate of flavours invoked by Onyx, and an interesting element of Atrium's cosmopolitan approach.
When I drive back home from Marche-en-Famenne, this brewday resonates in my head, for a brief moment letting me believe I have also journeyed to different parts of the world.

WHAT DOES 'CRAFT BREWING' MEAN TO YOU?

Paula: 'To us craft brewing means that you choose your brewing ingredients with love, in order to make the beer you want to brew, and not with a calculated price in your head. A craft brewer should brew to astonish people. And to do that he or she should brew with love. Onyx is an expensive beer to make, an all-grain imperial stout with 18 different types of malts and grains. It's also a difficult beer to make, requiring a lot from our brewhouse with its heavy grist and the high-gravity brewing technique we use. But we love this beer and so we brew it and don't want to go for less.'

ATRIUM BRASSERIE ARTISANALE
—
WWW.BRASSERIEATRIUM.BE
RUE DES BRASSEURS 9,
6900 MARCHE-EN-FAMENNE

THE SIGNATURE BEERS OF ATRIUM BRASSERIE ARTISANALE

Atrium opened its doors at the end of 2018 and started right away with six beers: The One (saison), Clémentine (wheat beer), Pam! (pale ale), Avalanche (IPA), Carya (brown ale) and Onyx (imperial stout). After a few months three new beers were added: Chihuahua (session IPA), Sombra (black IPA, a collab with Brasserie de la Sambre) and Onyx Amburana (barrel-aged imperial stout).
The beers are all-grain, with no sugar added to boost the alcohol. Atrium focuses on fresh ingredients and a cosmopolitan approach that reflects the brewers' background. Although all beers are dear to Paula and Valéry, asked to select three signature beers they choose the pale ale, the IPA and the imperial stout.

PAM!
(5.9% ABV)

This pale ale is a good example of how different brewing influences come together in one beer. For Pam! Paula and Valéry use English malts, American hops and a Belgian ale yeast, quite untypical for the style. It is a way to give it some recognisable features for their Marchois customers.
Pam! pours a copper-like amber with a white head. The aroma contains a touch of citrus, but is mainly floral with prominent pine notes. On the palate it starts with a subtle citrus acidity, followed by a herbal, floral and pine-like character and a bitter finish.

AVALANCHE
(6.8% ABV)

In this red IPA you can expect an avalanche of hop flavours, the result of multiple hopgifts at different stages of the boil and dry-hopping at primary and secondary fermentation.
The result is a red amber beer with an off-white foamy head that displays rich aromas of grapefruit, stonefruit and pineapple, and a floral backdrop. I can taste some malty sweetness at first, complemented by an outspoken, lingering hop bitterness. In this way Avalanche introduces a touch of the American West Coast to the Belgian Ardennes.

ONYX
(11% ABV)

Onyx is a pitch black imperial stout named after the precious black quartz-like mineral. Along with 15 different malts and grains, orange peel, vanilla and cocoa are among the ingredients in this rich, complex and sturdy beer. Elements of vanilla, chocolate and coffee define the aroma. On the tongue Onyx starts with a sweet bang, which gradually gives way to more bitter, roasted flavours. The strength of Onyx then finally unveils itself through a warming glow in crescendo. If Paula ever suffers from the Belgian cold again, she will probably drink an Onyx instead of raising the thermostat.

Honest, all-grain, no shortcuts

CRAFT PILSNER

Pilsners and lagers are without a doubt the most popular beer styles in the world. The only problem is they have a bad reputation for being bland, watery and full of cost-reducing adjuncts. Still, they played a vital role in the American craft beer revolution.

'Reinventing' the beer style that made the 'corporate enemy' so big probably was the best way to show what craft beer brewing is all about: making honest, flavourful all-grain beer without shortcuts to the final result. That's what many early American craft brewers did, Brooklyn Lager and Boston Lager being some of the best-known examples.

Sounds like pilsners and lagers are the perfect beers for homebrewing. Well, not exactly. They may be plain, straightforward beers, but they're not easy to brew. The point at which the brewer leaves the job to yeast and time, in particular, is where failure lurks around the corner.

Most lager yeast strains are delicate 'beings'. They need a more precise and lower temperature range than ale yeasts to do their job the way we want it done: a good, clean fermentation without a yeasty character, allowing the subtle malt character and noble hop flavours to shine in a crisp, crystal clear beer. Room temperature works perfectly well for ale yeast strains, but is troublesome for lager strains. Room temperatures are the perfect condition for a lager abundant in unwanted esters and off-flavours like diacetyl. And that you don't want!

Frigid Marie

The perfect temperature to ferment lagers is between 8 and 12°C (some strains endure temperatures up to 15°C). That's lower than room temperature and higher than the temperature of a fridge. Do you have a fridge at home that you can perfectly tune to a desired temperature? No? A cellar with a constant temperature? Nope? Me neither. Well, you can wait until winter to brew like in the old days. Or maybe you can try to buy a Bavarian alpine cave.

A customised fridge could be a solution, but it's costly or requires some technical skills that I don't have. My bathtub turned out to be the answer. And a freezer constantly filled with 20 or so bottles of frozen water to control the temperature of the water in which I put the fermentation bucket. It was like the mirror version of the bain marie: a frigid version of Marie's bathtub.

To maintain the desired temperature range — let's say around 12°C — fill your bathtub with water, about 30 cm high. Put the fermentation tank in the tub and surround it with plastic bottles filled with frozen water. Make sure you monitor the temperature well. By adding or removing bottles you should be able to make the water temperature a stable 12°C. When the temperature starts rising, replace the bottles of melting water with new ones straight from the freezer. It's not perfect and quite labour-intensive, and I would not recommend brewing a pilsner on hot summer days, but this bathroom method will prevent the fermentation process from 'spinning out of control'.

After a week let the temperature rise to 16°C and keep it at that temperature for another two weeks. Depending on the time of year and the conditions inside your house — an unheated room on the north side of your house should do — you won't be needing ice any more.

Rye session pilsner

Why rye in a pilsner? Mainly because rye gives more complexity and body to a beer and has refreshing qualities, characteristics we can use in a session pilsner to compensate for less alcohol.

FOR 11 LITRES PILSNER

MALT: *1.8 kg of pilsner malt, 150 g of rye malt, 150 g of flaked rye*
HOP: *14 g of Challenger, 15 g of Hallertau Perle and 45 g of Saaz*
YEAST: *lager yeast (Saflager S-23 or W34/70, Lager M76 or M84)*
EXTRA: *Irish moss*

MASH

— Add 16 litres of water to a kettle and attach the brewbag to the handles of the kettle. Warm up the water to 64°C.

90' —— Pour in the milled malts. The water will drop in temperature to about 63°C. Hold at 63°C for 60 minutes. If necessary, keep on stirring the malts while adjusting the temperature.

75' —— Adjust pH to 5.4.

25' —— Heat up to 72°C and hold for 20 minutes.

05' —— Heat up to 78°C.

— Pull out the bag, let it drain. You should be able to start the boil with 15 litres of wort with a pre-boil original gravity of 1030.

BOIL

70' —— Start to boil the wort. Just before it starts boiling adjust pH to 5.2.

60' —— Boil for 60 minutes. Add Challenger (14 g).

45' —— Add Hallertau Perle (5g) and Saaz (5 g).

30' —— Add Hallertau Perle (5g) and Saaz (5 g).

15' —— Add Hallertau Perle (5g) and Saaz (5 g).

10' —— Add Irish moss.

00' —— Add Saaz (30 g). Stop the boil.

FERMENTATION

— Cool down the wort to 25°C.
— Measure the specific gravity of the wort. You should reach an original gravity of 1041.
— Transfer to the fermentation bucket. About 11 litres should go into the bucket. Sprinkle the dry yeast over the wort.

- Let it ferment for a week at 12°C.
- After a week let the temperature rise to 16°C and keep it at that temperature for another two weeks.
- Final gravity should be around 1010 (approximately 4% ABV).

LAGERING

- Transfer the beer to the lagering bucket.
- Don't transfer the sediment: for a pilsner this is even more important than for the other beer styles. You're better off losing a litre more than ending up with a hazy pilsner.
- Lagering is the key element to make a good pilsner. The name for the beer style is derived from the German word '*lagern*', which originally meant 'to store' and today translates as 'to mature'.

BOTTLING AND BOTTLE CONDITIONING

- Boil 80 g of sugar (8 g per litre) in a small amount of water. Let it cool down to 25°C.
- Remove the bags with hops from the bucket and add the sugar water. Gently stir it with a sanitised spoon.
- Close the lid. You're ready to start bottling.
- Put the bottles in a warm dark place for a week in order to carbonate the beer. Then let it rest in a fridge. Patience is a virtue for this beer. It gets better when 'lagered' for a while, say about a month or two, before you crack a bottle.

BREWING NOTES

- If you want to brew this beer in summer, the bathtub trick won't be reliable or too labour-intensive and energy-devouring. If you stubbornly still brew this beer with lager yeast, you can let it spin out of control and call it a steam beer, like the historic lager that wasn't a lager from San Francisco.
- Or try a clean ale yeast instead, like US-05, to make a 'fake' pilsner, aiming at the same clean yeast profile, subtle malt character, herbal hop notes and dry finish.
- Or you can just brew another beer.

'WE'RE HAVING FUN'

Lanterne — pale ale
A dry-hopped, barrel-aged saison with Romanella

L'ERMITAGE NANO-BRASSERIE

'Hello, my name is Armando.' Armando? I haven't met the three brewers of L'Ermitage Nanobrasserie yet, we've only communicated via email, but I'm quite sure none of them is called Armando. And I always do my homework.

I introduce myself to Armando and greet his fellow brewer, who is inspecting the inside of the mash tun. When he lifts his head he replies: 'Ah, you must be here for the book. Hi, I'm Henri Bensaria.' This name sounds familiar to me. 'And this is Armando Romito from Maestri del Sannio. He's from the region around Naples and we're doing a collab today. But right now we're in the middle of brewing a batch of Lanterne.'

I recognise Henri. I've seen a video on YouTube from 2017 in which he introduces the then new city brewery in Anderlecht, Brussels. It's walking distance from the railway station of Brussels-South and one block away from one of Belgium's most internationally renowned breweries, Cantillon. Brewer Jean Van Roy is said to pop in on Friday nights to close off a working week with a L'Ermitage beer. A nice symbol for the state of beer affairs in Belgium: a beer institute and a newbie, a brewery embodying tradition and a brewery of the new wave, side by side.

Nele and I have arrived here by train. We're walking from the station to the brewery. Nele is limping, using crutches because of a knee injury after a skiing accident, and I'm carrying a bag with my rubber boots. Still, the train was more convenient than negotiating Brussels' traffic. And the short walk from the station to the Anderlecht neighbourhood passes through a lively and interesting part of the city.

L'Ermitage Nanobrasserie is housed in an old cigarette factory, a building that previously also offered workspace to artists and contains different layers of spaces. One part of the building is used for the brewhouse and the bottling line. Another part is the taproom, with wall paintings and DIY benches and tables made of OSB panels and pallets. It's exuding an urban atmosphere that recurs in almost everything the guys of L'Ermitage do.

NOT THE EASY ROAD

Fellow brewer Nacim Menu has joined us and guides Nele and me to the taproom, where we have an introductory chat about the brewery and the brewday. The brewing story of Nacim Menu, Henri Bensaria and François Simon, three real *Brusseleirs* or *Bruxellois*, starts when they were sharing a house in the Rue de l'Ermitage in Ixelles, one of Brussels' municipalities. All three have a background in visual arts or language studies. Nacim studied film directing, Henri studied Arab languages and François has a degree in advertising. And they shared a passion for beer, which led to some initial homebrewing experiments in 2013. The hobby quickly expanded, from playing around with a variety of styles to perfecting their recipes. They started in their kitchen and quite quickly moved to their cellar to brew 100 litre batches. The idea of making a living out of brewing was planted.

The styles they liked when they started brewing are the ones they still brew today, largely influenced by the popular American craft beer styles, but with their own interpretation. Nacim, Henri and François prefer beers that are easy to drink, not too high in alcohol, hop-forward and well balanced. Their artistic and urban background is also visible in the beer labels, designed and drawn by their friend Krump in a postmodern graphic style, based on the tarot tradition from Marseille. The labels depict a hermit, referring to the brewery's name and its origins in the Rue de l'Ermitage (Hermitage Street), or the brewers.

It all seems to contrast with the rural approach of Armando Romito and his project Maestri del Sannio. Although L'Ermitage have made saisons before and are starting a saison project as we speak, from my outside perspective I wouldn't link their beers to the Belgian tradition or an organic approach with the use of long-lost ingredients. But it turns out I'm completely wrong.

A little while ago Henri spent a week in Cerreto Sannita, Armando's hometown in Campania, about one hour from Naples. He and Armando brewed together, and Armando showed Henri the region, including tourist hotspots like Rome. The Eternal City 'invited' them to spend a wild night there, which became the inspiration for the name of their collab beer: Cuvée Henri Street Sleeper, a dry-hopped barrel-aged saison. The bottle label shows a collage of pictures, one of which shows Henri asleep on a Roman street. The slogan above his head reads: 'Wherever life may lead you'.

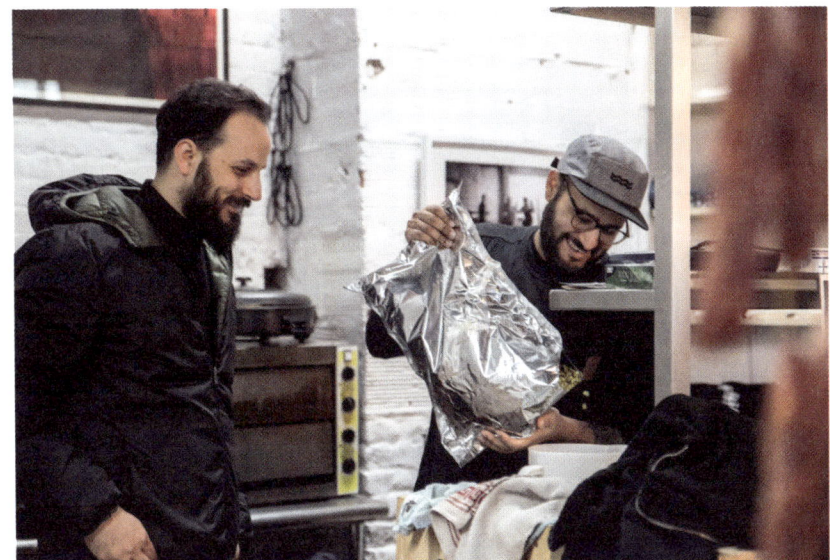

As I get to witness these guys throughout the day it appears to me this slogan is probably what connects them. In the case of Nacim, Henri and François it means that they came across a new passion and decided to go all the way with it, despite a lack of expertise through schooling and the huge financial risk they would have to take. Nacim: 'We started from scratch, without a professional background or money. That's rarely a winning combination.' That's why they first started to brew professionally at Brasserie de Bastogne (today Brasserie Minne) and in the meantime worked out their financial plan and contacted banks to get a business loan. In 2017 they brewed here for the first time.

The least you can say is that the three founders of L'Ermitage don't shy away from taking a risk. The path Armando took isn't the easiest one either. With Maestri del Sannio he's passionately making beers with Romanella, an ancient wheat variety from the Campania region. Ancient wheat varieties like Romanella are not easy to get, not even in Armando's home area. They are grown by a limited number of local organic farmers. And they haven't been modified for brewing like most malts. It means that brewing with grains like Romanella is more labour-intensive. For one thing it may cause some problems during the brewing process. And it is less cost-effective. But that's not any of these guys' concern today — it hardly ever is with collabs, the experience being the main goal.

THE MILLIONAIRE, THE CROCODILE AND THE EMPEROR

Today three brew sessions are planned: one for Lanterne, L'Ermitage's pale ale, and two batches of the collab saison with Romanella. The rest of the malt bill contains pilsner malt, spelt and oatmeal flakes. Some bitter hops will be added early in the boil. Once fermented with a very fruity saison yeast — a strain appropriately called Fruit Bomb Saison — the beer will be aged in red wine barrels and then dry-hopped.

Armando actually wanted to bring durum wheat with him as well, but the bags got lost in transport. 'The durum wheat was lost, but the Romanella came through and so it has survived twice: this week in transit to Brussels, and, more importantly, from vanishing entirely as a wheat variety.'

By now Henri has transferred the batch of Lanterne to the brewkettle and Nacim has emptied and cleaned the lauter tun. He starts filling it with water for the next batch. On the other side of the brewhouse Nicolas, L'Ermitage's only employee, is cleaning one of the fermentation tanks. Water is flowing from one of the valves, on the floor and then towards the drain. I try to make myself useful by wiping the floor, but Nicolas tells me I'd better wait because more water will follow anyway and all my wiping efforts will come to nothing.

It's nearly 11 a.m. and time to start preparing the first batch of the collab saison. Having fun and learning new things may be at the heart of a collab session, but efficiency is at the heart of L'Ermitage's operating method. Running a brewery is more than just brewing beer, and in small breweries the brewer is supposed to be a jack-of-all-trades. That's why the week planning in L'Ermitage only consists of two brewdays, during which three batches of 800 litres are brewed. Not a second is wasted. Well... Only if you call a short coffee break while tasting a recently brewed beer a waste of time.

Henri brings us a tasting glass with a coffee stout that's simply called Coffee Stout. It's a one-off beer, based on a recipe by one of L'Ermitage's interns, and the fourth beer of La Laboratoire d'Alchimie, a series in which the three brewers push their boundaries. While I'm smelling and tasting the beer, Nacim, Henri and Armando go through the brewing schedule — François has a half day off and will arrive around noon for the next batch.

Armando explains to me that ancient wheat varieties like Romanella contain more proteins. 'We will start with a protein rest in between 52 and 57°C to break down protein chains. It helps to improve lautering and makes the beer a little less hazy.'

While Armando helps Nacim to pour the milled grains (malted and unmalted) in the mash tun I take a look around. I notice a new beer running down the bottling line. I recognise it as a L'Ermitage beer because of the trademark Krump labels. It's a double IPA called Suske le Millionaire, with Cryo Hops (aromatic hop lupulin powder) and passion fruit purée. It's what François will later describe to me as a birthday beer, unaware that I saw 'his beer' being bottled while he wasn't present.

Coffee Stout break. Hardly a waste of time.

François — Suske in the Brussels dialect — made the recipe for the beer, Nacim and Henri thought of the name and the design of the label and will reveal this at a public event in L'Ermitage's taproom on François' birthday. For the other two brewers' birthdays the same way of working was applied. Henri's birthday beer was called Crocodile Henri, a cream ale. Nacim's was a pale ale called Nacimilien d'Autriche, a pun referring to Maximilian of Austria, a historic ruler of the Burgundian-Habsburg dynasty and later emperor of the Holy Roman Empire, whose seat of power around 1500 was Brussels. The puns in the beer names are exemplary. These guys really don't want to let business interfere with their friendship. *'On s'amuse,'* François tells me in the afternoon. 'We're having fun.'

Being playful, however, does not exclude hard work. Nacim and Henri are busy bees. And when François joins them he turns out to be no different. There is a coming and going of the three of them, almost tuned to the rhythm of the punk rock that is blasting out of a boombox in the corner of the brewhouse. It seems a little unstructured, but with every step in the process one of the three brewers shows up on time, almost out of nowhere. They each know what part to play when, and if necessary they put their heads together.

AFTERNOON TEA TIME WITH BEER AND OREGANO

In collabs the host brewer always takes the lead. Because in this situation there are three brewers there isn't much work to do for Armando (or for me for that matter). Time for him to do what an Italian does like no one else, even if he's a brewer: making pizza. He takes me to the kitchen in the back of the taproom and lifts a towel from a baking tray. It's filled with pizza dough that has this lovely smell of baker's yeast. 'I made this dough yesterday night. It's perfect by now. You know, the funny thing is, yesterday I bought olive oil for the first time in my life. And passata. My dad makes his own olive oil and passata. But I forgot to buy oregano. We always have fresh oregano at home.'

Because all I can do for now is observe while I actually crave to play a more active role, I offer to go and buy some oregano in a nearby grocery store. He welcomes the idea enthusiastically. 'No good pizza marinara without oregano,' he says with fervour. Armando explains to me the importance of the herb for an authentic Neapolitan pizza like the marinara, which excels in simplicity, with the only ingredients being pizza dough, marinara sauce, garlic, oregano and olive oil. A limited number of quality ingredients for a lot of flavour. It sounds a lot like the beers he and the guys from L'Ermitage like to brew.

When I get back with the oregano I first have a look at the brewing activity. Lautering is finished and Nacim has started to pump the wort to the brewkettle, but the transfer pipe is clogged, most likely because of the Romanella. Nacim stays calm and doesn't force anything. I decide not to look over his shoulder and go to the kitchen to give Armando the oregano.

He is making preparations for a pizza margherita. I see some freshly plucked basil in a glass of water. 'If you put the stems of the basil leaves in some water they stay fresh for a while.'

L'Ermitage makes beer with passion fruit, tea, grapefruit juice... No Bavarian purity laws for them. I wonder whether basil would work in beer too. 'They do it in Italy,' Armando tells me. 'And I think Mikkeller has made a beer with basil too,' says Henri who has joined us in the kitchen. A quick search on the internet tells me Mikkeller's basil beer in fact was the result of a collab with Lindemans called Spontanbasil, a lambic with fresh basil.

We're well past noon when the first pizza is served. As you probably remember, the rhythm of a day at a brewery is determined by the brewing schedule, not the other way around. Because the transfer from the lauter tun to the brewkettle went slower than expected, lunch was postponed. It wasn't the first time that lunch was a lot like afternoon tea time. Anything for good beer!

The pizza is delicious, as is the Lanterne I drink with it. The tropical aromas and flavours and the subtle floral notes are a good match with the marinara sauce and the oregano. A Hawaiian pizza without actually committing blasphemy.

From where I sit at the bar, holding a slice of pizza, I can see a poster on the door with all the labels of the beers brewed from October 2017, when L'Ermitage opened the brewery in Anderlecht, to October 2018. In their first year 24 beers saw the light of day, which is crazy in terms of most business model standards. But for L'Ermitage it works.

'Our beers are made by *Brusseleirs* for *Brusseleirs*.' The local approach could be the explanation for L'Ermitage's success. Brussels has several new breweries now, all doing well. 'We can't keep up with the demand,' François says. 'We would like to keep the capacity limited, because we don't have any real growing ambitions. So we try to get more out of our brewing installation to meet the demand, but everytime we do we receive more orders than before.'

One of their plans for the near future is to start a beer bar in the centre of Brussels. 'Mostly because we would like to have better control over our distribution and be closer to the people who drink our beers.'

L'Ermitage Nanobrasserie found a home in an old cigarette factory, a building that previously also offered workspace to artists.

Sounds like a great plan. There's more than enough room in Brussels, and Belgium, for bars and breweries where you can drink beers that are interesting, original, great, or all of these characteristics combined. Beers that were made head first, without a safety net, by a local, passionate brewer. Or brewers. Three of them.

WHAT DOES 'CRAFT BREWING' MEAN TO YOU?

Nacim: '"Craft" to us is summarised in three key words: independence, proximity and authenticity.'

L'ERMITAGE NANOBRASSERIE
—
ERMITAGENANOBRASSERIE.BE
RUE LAMBERT CRICKX 26,
1070 ANDERLECHT

THE SIGNATURE BEERS OF L'ERMITAGE

L'Ermitage has four beers that are available all year round. These signature beers are complemented with seasonal variations, one-shots and more experimental beers featuring in La Laboratoire d'Alchimie. The purpose of this huge range of beers is to navigate through a variety of beer styles. And then there are those beers Nacim, Henri and François make for fun, like the birthday beers. In their first year it all added up to 24 beers.

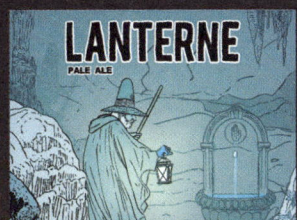   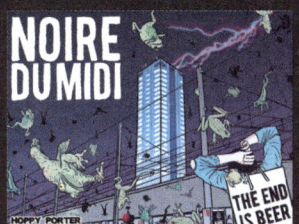

LANTERNE
(5% ABV)

Lanterne is the first beer L'Ermitage released. They first brewed it at Brasserie de Bastogne and in October 2017 it was the first beer they brewed in their new brewhouse. Lanterne is an easy-drinking, light pale ale with Mosaic and Cascade hops. The tropical fruits from Mosaic dominate the nose. When the glass gets some air, though, a floral, slightly earthy aroma typical of Cascade follows. Tropical fruits are also the first flavour impression, followed by a resinous accent and a lingering hop-bitter finish.

SOLEIL
(4.5% ABV)

The Soleil bottle was the first beer to showcase the work of graphic artist Krump, who has since designed all the L'Ermitage beer labels.
Soleil is a refreshing, thirst-quenching session wheat ale that looks hazy, with a very light yellow colour and a creamy head with large bubbles. The aroma displays grapefruit, pineapple and tangerine. The first sip gives a fresh, well-carbonated, soft-bitter impression with a light acidity from the wheat. The finish is dry, drier than one would expect from a wheat ale, unveiling similarities with a crisp saison or a dry pale ale.

THÉORÈME DE L'EMPEREUR
(6.4% ABV)

This pale ale with jasmine tea is golden, almost orange in appearance and pours a frothy white head with good head retention. The aroma is rich and complex with elements of stone fruit and citrus from the hops, and with a jasmine perfume, giving it the occidental touch suggested on the label. Although 6.4% ABV, this pale ale goes down easily, with some sweetness at first, then a lot of fruity and floral notes, ending moderately bitter. Théorème de l'empereur would pair well with a medium-spiced world kitchen full of fresh herbs.

NOIR DU MIDI
(6.9% ABV)

The name of this hoppy porter refers to its colour — 'noir' means 'black' in French, the colour of a porter or stout — and the part of Brussels that is home to L'Ermitage, le Midi or the South. In a hoppy porter a subtle fruitiness is no surprise. It is seeping through the mainly roasted aromas. The fruitiness from the hops also returns on the palate, followed by a spicy, roasty flavour with notes of chocolate. It ends in gentle bitterness from the roasted malts.

Thinking outside the box

BEER-CIDER HYBRID

Craft brewers love the challenge of creating a near infinite gamut of beers using only the basic ingredients water, malt, hop and yeast. But for many of them the search for new recipes, techniques and, ultimately, beers doesn't stop at... beer.

Craft brewers are very wary of using adjuncts, especially if these would come across as adjuncts used to reduce costs or to take a shortcut in the brewing process. On the other hand, for some craft brewers no adjunct is too out there. Beer with cucumber? Sounds weird, but if done well it actually makes for refreshing beer. Chilli peppers? A great combination with roasted malts in porters and stouts. In fact, anything from curry spices, through mustard seeds to meat have been used in beer that still tastes like beer.

Some ingredients one wouldn't automatically associate with beer are no longer considered alien to it. Oyster shells in an oyster stout or coffee in a coffee stout are very common and widely accepted by beer lovers. But some ingredients will remain crazy, even though they are closer to the essence of beer than you'd think. Like the yeast captured from Rogue Ales brewmaster John Maier's beard to make Beard Beer. In theory this wild yeast doesn't differ from any other captured wild yeast. But the idea...

Pushing the boundaries of beer is not necessarily about using wacky ingredients. It may also be a matter of crossing the boundaries between styles, drinks and traditions. Italy is traditionally a wine country, but it has a growing and thriving craft beer scene. Italian brewers brew great and interesting beers, and some cross the boundaries with wine, making Italian grape ale. The grape ale is often made by fermenting a mix of wort and grape juice, both sources of fermentable sugars. A more daring method, closer to spontaneous fermentation, is to mix the wort with squashed grapes. The grape skin is home to wild yeast that will ferment the wort and the grape juice.

Appleocalyptic

America loves beer… and cider. Both are historically favourite drinks of the common people and the many American farmers. This idea inspired Stephen King to invent a beer-cider hybrid called graf for his roaming characters in *The Dark Tower* series, a story set in an apocalyptic, western-like fantasy world.

In his novels King doesn't describe what graf is, other than an 'apple-beer', but online you can find all kinds of interpretations of graf (often spelled graf) made by homebrewers. A commercial example would be GRAFF(T), the result of a collab between New Belgium, Two Beers Brewing and Seattle Cider Company. GRAFF(T) is an India pale lager with apple must accounting for 10%.

Using apples in beer isn't new and not limited to any style or method. While graf and GRAFF(T) mix wort and apple juice to ferment together, the 10 Apple Stout, a collab beer of To Øl from Denmark and Põhjala Brewery from Estonia, uses ten different ways to integrate the aroma and flavours of ten apple species into this barrel-aged imperial stout of 12% ABV.

Hoppy beer-cider hybrid

This recipe is for a graf-inspired beer-cider hybrid or apple ale. Because this is a book about beer and most grafs tend to be either 50% beer and 50% cider, or even more cider than beer, I've sized down the amount of apple juice to about 20%. This beer should be refreshing, mildly bitter and a little tart, giving a slight impression of spontaneous fermentation (which it did not).

FOR
11 LITRES
BEER-CIDER HYBRID

MALT: *2.7 kg of pilsner malt*
HOP: *15 g of East Kent Goldings, 30 g of Hallertau Perle, 30 g of Groene Bel, 40 g of El Dorado*
YEAST: *SafAle US-05*
EXTRA: *Irish moss, 2 litres of organic apple juice*

MASH

— Add 16 litres of water to a kettle and attach the brewbag to the handles of the kettle. Warm up the water to 64°C.

90' —— Pour in the milled malts. The water will drop in temperature to about 63°C.
Stir the malts to avoid clumps. Hold at 63°C for 60 minutes.

80' —— Adjust pH to 5.4.

30' —— Heat up to 72°C and hold for 20 minutes.

— Pull out the bag, let it drain. You should be able to start the boil with 15 litres of wort with a pre-boil original gravity of 1042.

BOIL

70' —— Start to boil the wort. Just before it starts boiling adjust pH to 5.2.

60' —— Boil for 60 minutes. Add East Kent Goldings (15 g).

10' —— Add Irish moss (5g).

00' —— Add Hallertau Perle (30 g) and Groene Bel (30 g). Stop the boil.

FERMENTATION

— Cool down the wort to 25°C.
— Measure the specific gravity of the wort. You should reach an original gravity of 1058.
— Pour 2 litres of unfiltered organic apple juice without additives into the fermentation bucket. Then add the wort (you will have about 10 litres: 11 litres after the boil minus 1 litre of trub) and sprinkle the dry yeast over it. Read the original gravity again (it will probably have dropped a bit, because most store-bought apple juice is around 1050).
— Let it ferment for a week at around 18–20°C. Final gravity should be around 1008 (approximately 6–6.5% ABV, depending on the original gravity of the apple juice).

LAGERING AND DRY-HOPPING

— Transfer the beer to the lautering bucket.
— Dry-hop with El Dorado (40 g) and let it lager for another week in a cooler place.

BOTTLING AND BOTTLE CONDITIONING

— Boil 80 g of sugar (8 g per litre, we want fairly high carbonation) in a small amount of water. Let it cool down to 25°C.
— Remove the bags with hops from the bucket and add the sugar water. Gently stir it with a sanitised spoon. Close the bucket again and you're ready to start bottling.
— Put the bottles in a warm dark place for a week in order to carbonate the beer. Then let it rest for another week in a cooler place or a fridge. For the hoppy version of the beer, drink it quite soon after bottling; for a more pronounced dry and tart character give it some time.

BREWING NOTES

— The head disappears quickly, probably from the apple juice. Looks more like cider than beer.
— First aromas are from El Dorado, but like in many hopped ciders they quickly disappear and give way to cider notes.
— In a next batch I would try some flaked barley and/or Carafoam for more mouthfeel and head retention, and some crystal malt to bring more balance and depth to the flavour profile.

'LIKE A FARMER WORKING IN THE FIELD, A BREWER NEEDS TO GET HIS HANDS DIRTY'

ANTIDOOT WILDE FERMENTEN

L'Or du pré — wild fermentation saison with dandelions

It's a bright morning, the first signs of a beautiful April summerlike day, when I arrive at Antidoot, the wild fermentation project of Tom and Wim Jacobs in the Flemish Brabant village of Kortenaken. Antidoot is best known for its wild fermentation beers, but Tom and Wim also make natural cider and wine. The farmhouse brewery is right next to Tom's house. It's the only 'homebrewery' I visit for this book and to Tom it's an integral part of a larger project in which he tries to live a life of self-sufficiency.

When I look inside the brewery it looks like nobody's there, so I ring the bell at Tom's house. His daughter Juno opens the door and knows right away I'm here for Antidoot. As an experienced host — later Tom tells me the larger part of his sales happen here at home, so his children are quite used to visitors — she guides me to the upper floor of the brewery. Tom is halfway inside a fermentation tank, cleaning the inside with a soft sponge. No wonder he didn't hear me a few minutes ago.

'I don't like to use cleaning chemicals too much,' Tom tells me. Brewing is mostly cleaning, but doing it the way Tom does tops everything. The first half hour I'm here, he will be going in and out of the tank with his head and upper body several more times. If you don't want to CIP all the time, you need to do some extra manual cleaning and you have to check whether anything remains on the tank walls. Tom does so using a flashlight and twisting to all sides in order to inspect every bend and curb on the inside of the conic tank.

A DEBUT WITH A BANG

Tom is preparing the tank for a transfer of wort for L'Or du pré, Antidoot's sour saison-style signature beer. The 2018 edition of L'Or du pré or 'Meadow's gold' had been highly anticipated by beer geeks and fans of wild and spontaneous fermentation even before it was available for the first time. Because Tom and Wim had already made a name with a lot of tastings, this was also the case for their summer 2018 release of a cider, the first product they sold when Antidoot officially got started. It was a debut with a bang. And more was to come: in 2019 Antidoot was elected Brewer of the Year 2018 at the Belgian Beer Awards Digital Festival.

The wort for L'Or du pré has been cooling down in a coolship for 16 hours and it has become a welcoming host to some wild microorganisms by now, coming from different sources in the brewery.

A roof made of vine branches from Tom's own vineyard is hanging over the coolship, its ornament a lamb's skull, symbol of medieval alchemy. However, the vine structure is not there for decoration. The ceiling, which is made of stainless steel plates, doesn't contain any microorganisms. Great news for most breweries, but Tom wants to have a thriving microculture to 'infect' the cooling wort. 'The branches carry their own microorganisms, such as wild yeasts. And the lime walls and the wooden barrels are welcoming guests for microbiological life as well. But I have to say the inspectors of the Federal Agency for the Safety of the Food Chain needed to be persuaded before they gave the green light.'

Tom's youngest daughter, Danse, pops in to say hello. 'Yesterday, she and her sister and some friends helped to pick dandelions. Fifteen kilos, that's quite a lot.' The dandelions are floating in the coolship now, together with some hop cones. 'Yesterday Wim and I brewed the wort and we let it cool during the night in this coolship. It's actually an old winemaker's tub that I turned into a coolship. We're making a saison-style beer the way it was originally done. It will taste nothing like the hoppy saisons you find today. Up to the Second World War all saisons were sour ales and often blended, a lot closer to lambics and gueuzes.'

The fermentation tank is ready now, but in order to transfer the wort fluently from the coolship Tom has to take other precautions as well. Because of the flowers the hose and pump might easily get blocked. Tom has placed an improvised double filter in front of the drain hole and added a joint with a looking glass to the pump in order to continuously follow the flow of the wort. Inventive ideas Tom puts into practice, often with recyled material. The precautions can't prevent the filter from getting jammed with trub, though; this way of making beer is accompanied by all kinds of challenges.

Tom sprays some rubbing alcohol on his hands and then pulls trub out of the filter with his bare hands. 'You don't normally see this in a brewery. Brewers are panicky when it comes to touching anything with their bare hands. In wine or cider making this is very normal. If fermentation goes well there shouldn't be a problem. The other microorganisms won't stand a chance against the yeast cells.'

To brew with wild flowers you need to be inventive and willing to use your hands.

LIKE WILD SHEEP

Antidoot specialises in wild fermentation, either through spontaneous fermentation, like in their lambics, or by adding a yeast starter of a wild yeast culture Tom captured in his garden. 'With this type of beer I want fermentation to hit off right away,' he says about L'Or du pré. He has just fetched a glass bottle containing a yeast starter. 'I'm going to pitch this in the fermentation tank while it's being filled with the wort. I'm not just relying on the wild yeasts and bacteria already in the wort. With spontaneous fermentation the wild yeasts need more time to multiply and start a healthy fermentation.'

Whether spontaneous fermentation or fermentation with captured and cultivated wild yeast, this way of brewing requires a different, more labour-intensive approach. Mashing in particular is quite different. 'We do a three-step mash with temperature rests at 49°C and 54°C. At that point three quarters of the mash gets an additional rest at 73°C and for one quarter of the mash we raise the temperature to 84°C to stop enzyme activity. We want long chains of sugars so that the wild yeast cells don't eat it all in primary fermentation. We want to keep some sugars to be consumed inside the barrels. People say wild yeasts aren't as effective as lab-cultivated Saccharomyces, but in fact they eat greedily. They're quite like wild sheep. Wild sheep even eat nettles.'

Not only mashing is more complicated, boiling is effort- and time-consuming as well. 'We boil the wort for three full hours, in order to have more integrated flavour and because the aged hops we use need time to let go of their oils.' Tom hands me a glass with a sample of the wort. It smells great and it's fruitier than I expected. 'The fruitiness might be from the dandelion pollen,' he explains.

Most of the time Tom and his brother Wim brew together. In fact, they try to do so every Tuesday in winter time. While Wim still works as a gastroenterologist in the Jessa hospital in Hasselt, Tom has become a full-time brewer and cider and wine maker since September 2018. He's also running all the other aspects of the brewery, the orchard and the vineyard. It all adds up to long, laborious days, but not without joy. 'Doing this is demanding. And you can't add up all the working hours into the price for a bottle. But you get paid with the freedom to do what you really like to do for a living.'

Tasting a bottle is work, both for Tom and for me, even on a sunny day like today. But it's as pleasant as work can be, especially after we've just emptied and cleaned the coolship. It's noon and time for a break from the physical part of brewing. Tom pours me a glass of a lambic with a variety of red fruits from the garden. It's a bottle from a batch that hasn't been released. It doesn't taste any less, though, coming with rich fruitiness and a hint of almonds and vanilla to the nose. From this non-blended beer of spontaneous fermentation I would expect a strong acidity, but I'm surprised by how gently the sourness tickles the tongue.

SUZUKI ATTACK

We're sitting on a bench in front of the brewery, looking over Tom's property, a little paradise of biodiversity and a huge contrast with the many orchards I saw on the road to Kortenaken. The region is rich in fruit farmers, but most put quantity first, with straight rows of dwarf trees as a visual sign. It looks nothing like Tom's organically organised patch of land, with a playzone for the children that gradually moves into a vegetable garden and some islands of blackberry plants, which turn towards a vineyard and some hop trellises supporting a revitalised Belgian hop variety, Groene Bel. A little further from the house is some sheep pasture.

Spread all over Tom's land are standard-size fruit trees with apricots, plums, pears and, mostly, apples: ancient Belgian apple varieties and, since recently, also some French and English varieties, traditionally used for Norman and English cider. 'The apple juice of the French and English varieties contains more tannins and gives more bitterness to the cider,' Tom explains.

When we stroll through the garden he talks about the principles of permaculture. 'The basic idea is that you don't keep plants apart, that through mixed plantation you enhance biological diversity and have different plants reinforce one another so you don't need pesticides to protect crops and fruits. In theory it sounds perfect, in reality it is quite challenging, very labour-intensive. And risky.'

In 2017 Tom's fruit plants were victim to a Japanese fruit fly, *D. Suzukii*, commonly known as the Suzuki fruit fly, a non-native species without natural enemies. The fly lays its eggs in fruit that isn't protected by the use of sulfites. It eats through the fruit skin to get inside and in doing so starts a process of vinegar production, which makes the fruits rot. A lot of fruit, blackberries in particular, was lost, but Tom could save up to 75% of his grapes by wrapping cloth around the grape clusters. One by one...

'In the long run — I'm talking about a decade — enough natural enemies should be attracted to fence off large colonies of the Suzuki flies. But in the meantime the permaculture seems to enhance the problem. These flies find an abundance of food and hosts for their eggs from spring till autumn.'

TERROIR

Tom has had setbacks before, but will not give in. His approach, both in the garden and the brewery, is not a practical or economical one, it's based on principles and a way of life. Antidoot is part of a larger project of Tom and his wife, Kristien Justaert. Ten years ago they left the city of Leuven to step away from the wrong priorities that a busy city life imposes on people, young families in particular. With a move to the countryside Tom had the intention of building up a self-sufficient life.

Until recently Tom was able to get up to 90% of his family's fruit and vegetable consumption from his garden. He even produced his own meat, breeding lamb and chickens and slaughtering them with his own hands. But now that he's a full-time brewer he lacks the time to work in the garden as much as is required for self-sufficiency.

It's early afternoon now and I'm accompanying Tom on an exploration of this 'terroir'. We're going to handpick dandelions. About 15 kilos of them. Tom has bought another patch of land on which nothing but grass and dandelions grow. You can't get any closer to adding terroir flavour to a beer. The dandelion 'harvest' will be used tomorrow, when Tom brews another batch of L'Or du pré.

It doesn't mean he has given up on this plan. Brewing farmhouse ales, and making natural wine and cider, plays an important part in it. The homebrewery allows him to work hard but still be very present as a dad. His choice of ingredients allows him to remain as local as possible and make products with a strong terroir character. The only ingredients that are not from the immediate surroundings are the malts and grains, but Tom tries to compensate for that by using organic malts and grains only.

Tom loves to use herbs, plants, roots and bark in his beers, going back to medieval gruit beer tradition. He is both inspired by this old Flemish tradition, through extensive reading of historical sources, and by French fortified wines like Vermouth and Italian bitters like Amaro and alpine liqueurs. They were a source of inspiration for Gentiana Lutea, a lambic-like sour ale with yellow gentian as a bittering agent, much like the dandelions in L'Or du pré.

SPECULATION

Back inside Tom pours a glass of lambic-like beer straight from the barrel. It is still in first fermentation and tastes a bit sweet, still containing many sugars that haven't been turned into alcohol yet. I taste a lot of esters too. 'Don't drink too much, it might affect your bowels. In fact, drinking from beer in early fermentation isn't without risk. It may still contain some pathogens that haven't been repressed by the alcohol. But this one should be safe, being around 5% in alcohol already.'

I ask Tom whether he would consider himself a lambic and saison brewer, but he insists he is not. 'Although we're brewing farmhouse ales, on the label we don't call it a lambic or a saison. We describe what's inside the bottle but we don't use the terms for the beer styles. The styles are unimportant, not even interesting. Hybrids are more interesting.' Tom would like Antidoot to blur the lines further between beer and other fermented drinks. He wants to experiment with hybrids of beer and cider, for instance. 'Is it beer or cider? That's an interesting question. And to me a drink like that shouldn't even need to be carbonated. But Wim doesn't always agree with that.'

Whatever Tom would call his beers, he rarely brews them the same way twice and only produces low volumes. Today's batch of L'Or du pré, and the batch Tom will brew tomorrow, will mature in six barrels of 200 litres for between 12 and 18 months. For an Antidoot beer that is a large volume. 'Our yearly production volume would fit into one foeder of Boon's,' Tom says.

Brewing like this means bottles are quickly sold out and rare, becoming prone to speculation. 'A lot of money is paid for craft beers with limited availability. By beer geeks, but also by speculators. I recently discovered that someone who had bought an Antidoot magnum bottle on one of the tastings here tried to sell it for a huge profit through a raffle, a kind of online lottery organised in a closed Facebook group. I mailed him to tell him I can't accept that kind of practice.'

To round off this sunny day we drink a glass of Gentiana Lutea. Tom has also fetched me a bottle of last year's L'Or du pré, to taste at home. On the label the skull reappears, the symbol of medieval alchemy. Tom, who used to teach philosophy and ethics at the UCLL Hogeschool in Leuven, draws a lot of inspiration from the philosophy behind alchemy, which is reflected in the name 'Antidoot'.

'The name refers to an antidote, something to counteract a poison, such as the dictation of purity, a mantra for modern brewers, who sterilise everything. The big idea of this philosophy is that everything is circular, that what dies gives life. Compost is a good example. On a symbolic level it means you need to bite the bullet sometimes to achieve something.' Antidoot also sounds like 'anti-death' in Dutch. 'That sometimes leads to funny situations on the phone, when I call a supplier and introduce myself as Tom from "anti-death".'

Replenished with an antidote to the rat race, I drive back home. Around Brussels I end up in a traffic jam, but I decide not to worry about it. In my head I am still enjoying this inspiring day. At least until I need to focus on the road again.

WHAT DOES 'CRAFT BREWING' MEAN TO YOU?

Tom: 'I'm not sure where we fit in with the craft brewers. I see more similarities with natural wine and cider making than with what most brewers in the craft beer scene do, although I have a lot of friends in that scene. The thing is, the whole movement is a bit contradictory: against the big, capitalist breweries, the multinationals, on the one hand, and a symptom of globalism on the other: brewers brewing the same beer styles, using the same commercial, pure-culture yeast strains.

It's all too much part of a hype to me and too focused on recipe-building instead of growing one's own yeast strain, which I believe is the real source of diversity. Traditional brewers are often looked down upon for being old-fashioned, but many have worked hard and stubbornly on this one yeast strain to make this one beer. I miss that kind of steadfastness in the craft beer world.

The notion of "craft" somehow has eroded. To me brewing is a physical thing: like a farmer working in the field you need to get your hands dirty.'

ANTIDOOT WILDE FERMENTEN
—
ANTIDOOT.BE
DIESTSESTRAAT 41,
3470 KORTENAKEN

THE SIGNATURE BEERS OF ANTIDOOT

Antidoot don't have a fixed set of signature beers, but a signature style. 'We hardly ever make two beers exactly the same way. Although you could say that we vary on the spontaneous fermentation and wild yeast theme. We also play with variables like herbs, plants, roots or fruit, anything that's available in our immediate environment.'

A number of key elements in Antidoot's signature style are:

— spontaneous fermentation or fermentation with Antidoot's own wild yeast culture

— the limited use of hops. Nearly only aged hops are used to preserve the beers. Tom uses herbs and plants, like dandelions, to bitter and flavour his beers

— a strong influence from the world of natural wines and even cocktails, more than from other brewers and beers

— a 19th-century approach, from before the time when brewers became obsessed with hygiene.

To get your hands on an Antidoot beer you will have to follow Tom closely on Facebook and be quick to get your 'seat' on one of Antidoot's events. I was lucky that Tom could give me one of the last bottles of 2018's L'Or du pré to taste and describe it here. Antidoot's beers consistently come in 75 cl bottles. That's why I tasted this one in good company.

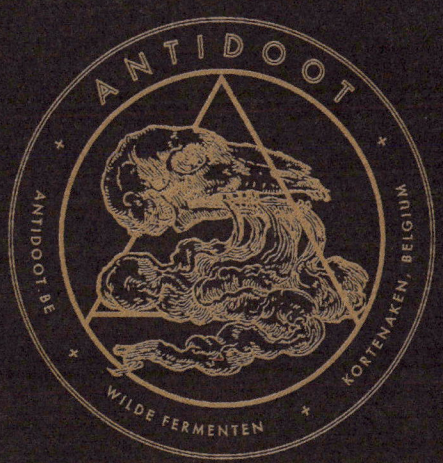

L'OR DU PRÉ
(6.6% ABV)

is made of malted barley, raw wheat and raw spelt, is sparsely hopped and contains dandelions, mainly for bittering and to contribute to a complex flavour. L'Or du pré is a golden blond, a bit hazy with a fine mousse under a thick white head. In the aroma I recognise notes of green apple, some floral elements from the dandelions and brett characteristics like horse blanket. This is a sour ale, but not an astringent one. The fruity acidity is well supported by a light, sparkling mouthfeel that turns dry towards the finish, with bitter final notes from the dandelions.

The hunt for the wild yeast

WILD YEAST FERMENTATION

If you want to brew the way they did in ancient times, you should go for spontaneous fermentation or capture wild yeast like a hunter-brewer.

The knowledge about what yeast is and what part it plays in the 'genesis' of beer was only achieved recently. In 1858 Louis Pasteur was the first to publish about fermentation processes and yeast. And it wasn't until 1883, when Emil Christian Hansen islotated a pure yeast cell, that lab-grown pure yeast strains became a possibility for brewers. To put this in perspective: the oldest traces of brewing go back 7000 years. Even the old practice of pitching yeast from one batch to another is a brewing method that is still in its infancy compared to spontaneous fermentation.

In the second half of the 20th century spontaneously fermented beers vanished almost entirely from the global beer market, exceptions being some beers from breweries near and in Brussels, in the Pajottenland and the larger Senne valley, where they continued to produce lambics and gueuzes. Today sour ales, spontaneously fermented beers in particular, are more popular than ever, especially because nowadays fans of sour beers are fans completely by their own free will and hence very devoted.

Coolship fever

For a long time there was this myth that lambics and gueuzes were only possible in the larger Senne valley, because of microorganisms in the air native to that region. Science shows that wild Saccharomyces, Lactobacillus, Pediococcus and Brettanomyces can be found everywhere. What makes lambics and gueuzes unique is the craft of these brewers and blenders that has been passed on for generations, and the tamed wild yeasts and bacteria inside their barrels, which enhance the effect of the wild yeasts and bacteria that overnight infected the wort in the coolship.

With the right amount of patience, skill and dedication, similar types of beer can be produced elsewhere in the world. The result will be different, as is the case with the different lambics and gueuzes from the Senne valley.

American craft brewers have always been happy to be inspired by Belgian beer traditions and quite a few breweries have built coolships, starting with Maine's Allagash Brewing Company in 2007. An article on Craftbeer.com even speaks about a coolship fever in America, naming Cantillon as the source of the virus.

Wild Brett cult

Spontaneous fermentation and the wild yeast species Brettanomyces in particular have a large fan base. Brettanomyces even has a nickname, Wild Brett. And because of its popularity this wild yeast has been cultured and is available to homebrewers too.

Signs of Wild Brett's popularity are the many beer festivals devoted to this one yeast species. Carnivale Brettanomyces, for instance, which takes place in different beer pubs in Amsterdam every summer and celebrates the qualities of Brettanomyces and other wild yeasts and bacteria alike. It's the festival where Antidoot started to build a name before they even released their first product. Brettanomyces is Greek for 'British fungus', which doesn't sound very appetising. That's not a coincidence, as it was first perceived as causing off-flavours. Today Brettanomyces is cherished by brewers and beer lovers, and it's gaining popularity among cider makers as well. Even wine makers of natural wines have come to appreciate Wild Brett.

What makes Brettanomyces so attractive to craft brewers is both its distinctive features, setting a brett beer apart from any other beer (think Orval), and its unpredictability, which makes a beer with Brett slightly different and surprising every time.

CAPTURING YOUR OWN WILD YEAST

- In essence capturing wild yeast from your own surroundings is quite simple and doesn't require much work or tools. The only catch is that the outcome is hard to predict and might as well be a complete failure.
- For a wild yeast starter, make 1 litre of wort, boiling 114 g of dried malt extract in 1.2 litres of water with 1 g of aged hops or hops low in alpha acids (you want the hops to make the wort less inviting to acid bacteria, not bitter it). Your wort will have an original gravity of approximately 1040.
- Pour into three or four sanitised jars (spread of risk), cover with cheese cloth or hop bags, having previously steamed the cloth or bags to sterilise them. Tighten the cloth around the jar with a rubber band.
- Put it outside for the night. Find a spot off the ground (out of reach for animals like cats) with as much airflow as possible.
- The next morning: bring it back inside and pour the wort into bottles. Seal each bottle with an airlock. If you haven't got bottles with an airlock, you can leave the wort in the jar and seal it with a freezer bag and rubber band. Let the bottles sit for a week or three. After a couple of days you should notice the first signs of fermentation.
- After three weeks you will be able to tell in which bottle (worst case all bottles) the wrong organisms are winning the battle, like fungi and black mould. Some white or green mold is okay. If the smell pleases you, just remove the mould with a sanitised spoon.
- Smell the bottles. If it really stinks, get rid of it. You're trying to catch wild yeast in order to brew beer based on (some sort of) spontaneous fermentation, which means that you like sour ales and you know what to expect from them in the nose. Look for the same aromas in your wild yeast starter, which will mainly be sour fruity and funky barnyard smells.
- A last test: remove the surface and take a sample. Pour in a glass. Does it look clear? Slightly hazy is ok. And now… taste it. If you like what you taste (but don't expect a well-balanced gueuze!), your wild yeast starter is ready to be used for a batch of beer.

NOTES

— The best period to harvest wild yeasts would be from autumn to spring, when temperatures at night are colder, so the wort can cool down quick enough to give the yeasts a head start and win over other microorganisms, like different species of acid bacteria, which thrive at higher temperatures.

— Once you are satisfied with the result of your propagated wild yeast, you can use it for instance in this simplified recipe and find out about the effects of your captured wild yeast. Use 1.6 kg of pilsner malt and 1 kg of wheat malt. Mash for 30 minutes at 62°C and 40 minutes at 72°C to create more non-fermentable sugars like dextrins. Boil for 60 to 90 minutes and only add 5 g of East Kent Goldings or Groene Bel (hops low in alpha acids) early on in the boil. If you are patient enough, Wild Brett will even devour those dextrins over time, adding its trademark aromas and flavour to your beer. That is if you have caught some Brettanomyces in the first place and if your beer is drinkable.

A wild yeast beer is a lot like the proverbial box of chocolates: you never know what you're gonna get.

— You should be aware that beers of wild or spontaneous fermentation become those well-balanced, complex sour ales we like through barrel-ageing and blending. And that's a different story. But it shouldn't keep you from playing with those wild yeasts you've captured.

— For more information on capturing and propagating wild yeast: check themadfermentationist.com and/or bootlegbiology.com

'WE WANT TO BE THIS PLACE WHERE PEOPLE FEEL FREE TO POP IN TO TASTE A BEER'

No crying over spilled malt —hoppy amber ale and brew test with leftover malts

CABARDOUCHE

'We are almost real brewers now, who can brew their own beers in their proper brewery.' It must have felt like ages for the Cabardouche brewers' collective. They had wanted to open their nanobrewery in March 2019, but because of an unfortunate accumulation of smaller and larger problems it took another five months before everything was ready for wort and beer to flow through the system.

A couple of months ago I visited the brewery-to-be during a shareholders' meeting. It was supposed to be a day to celebrate. To show shareholders in their new cooperative society limited — most if not all of them friends and relatives of the brewers — what their money had been used for. But delivery of the brewing equipment had been postponed. Not for the first time. Or the last. But they didn't know that yet.

When I arrive at the meeting today, Elise, with whom I have talked on the phone before, introduces me to her fellow brewers Igor, Jens, Stendert and Peter, and shows me around the renovated and decorated space under a railway arch at the Borgerhout Centers that will be their brewery. It's part of a larger city project, in which railway arches are renovated to become home to a variety of small businesses.

They've turned their arch or Center into a cosy meeting place, inviting to passersby. With the ground floor — chairs lined up for about 30 of the 67 shareholders, including the five brewers — and a mezzanine it's impressive how much room has been created in a place without space. Or is it because the mezzanine is still empty, lacking the equipment it is intended for?

One of the first things Elise points out to me is a system, as ingenious as it is primitive, to divert leaking water from the rail platform to the sewers. Through a gutter the water flows to two pipes that go through the wall on either side of the arch, where the water then trickles down the exterior walls. 'The developers of the site never considered that when it rains the water needs to find a way down from the rail platform and the railway tracks. It seeps through the different brick and concrete layers and ends up seeping through the ceilings of these railway arches. They have tried to solve the problem. Many more elegant solutions didn't work. The underlying problem isn't gone, but it will do for now. Maybe we should adjust a gargoyle to the pipes.' Elise apparently still sees the funny side of the problems that have slowed Cabardouche down.

This shareholders' meeting, like any, is accompanied by some formalities, one of them is the obligation to have a majority vote. My presence as an outsider, for instance, needs to be approved by all shareholders. Because this is a group of people well known to the brewers, the formalities are more like a source of laughter and are dealt with with a sense of irony. But a vote is a vote. And I'm allowed to stay.

INNUENDO

The first brewing plans of Cabardouche took off when five friends, who met on a beer connoisseur course, started to brew together at home. In 2012 Igor, Jens, Stendert, Peter and Elise began playing with a starter kit Peter had received as a gift and soon after participated in the Brouwland Biercompetitie with one of their first brews. 'We didn't win,' Peter says. 'Our beer tasted a bit like spaghetti sauce, because we used too many chilli peppers.'

The five brewers divide work tasks on brewdays. While Peter is measuring the wort's gravity, Elise and Stendert catch up on paperwork. But they never forget to enjoy the brewday.

But the excitement about brewing grew. They started to work on some recipes and began a quest for a name for the brewery and the future beers. 'Finding a good name wasn't easy, and looking back some names that made the shortlist sound a bit silly.' Puns are at the heart of so many beer names. And puns are a delicate form of humour. It was Cabardouche, an Antwerp slang term for a brothel, derived from French, that finally made it to the top of the list.

The names for the beers are related to that brothel innuendo: Blonde Stoot translates as 'blond hotty', Stout Mokke as 'naughty girl', Rosse Voenk as 'red-haired spark', and Escort Deluxe, well, speaks for itself.

In 2014 they took one of their recipes, an upgraded barrel-aged version of Rosse Voenk dubbed Escort Deluxe, to the Pirlot brewery in Zandhoven. Their first beer ready for consumers outside of their circle of friends and family was born. They would sell limited amounts of it as a Christmas and New Year's gift. To do that, they needed to become a beer company and decide about a company structure. Because making a profit was not the intention, and their connection with the Borgerhout district of Antwerp and local cultural life was essential, Cabardouche started as a non-profit organisation.

Blonde Stoot and Stout Mokke soon followed, the first one quickly becoming a success in Borgerhout. Apart from their own beers they also made beers for local initiatives, like Reus ('Giant') for the Borgerhout Reuzenstoet ('Giants' Parade'). As sales kept on growing and the plans to start their own brewery became more concrete, they also started a cooperative society limited for the brewing and beer-selling activities, allowing Cabardouche to make profits, reinvest, attract extra investments to start a physical brewery of their own and still maintain strong ties with the local community.

TO CONTRACT OR NOT TO CONTRACT

Given the growing demand for Cabardouche beers in Borgerhout and the larger Antwerp area, the brewers do not plan to brew all of their beers in their new brewery, once it's operational. 'We bought a brewing installation aimed at batches of 150 litres, plus two fermentation tanks of 150 litres and two fermentation tanks of 300 litres, in which we can ferment two consecutive batches. And yes, I know, that's still not very much,' Elise tells me. 'Instead of brewing our most popular beers ourselves, we want to focus on recipe development, trying new things all the time, and brewing on demand for local organisations and anyone who has got a great or crazy idea we can identify with.'

'We want to be a lot like the baker's just around the corner. When locals pop in there they get the lovely smell of freshly baked bread and get to choose from a variety of breads and pastries, and have a little chat. We want to be a similar place where people go to try a new beer just like they would buy croissants on a Sunday morning. We won't be a brewpub, but more of a brew shop/beer shop, although we hope that when the city project here at the Centers in Borgerhout expands we'll have more space and can have a terrace in front of the brewery.'

'We know that experimenting with new beers and recipes all the time will drive the excise duty inspectors crazy,' Elise continues. 'It's a concept that is fairly new and unusual to them. They're used to breweries with a limited number of beers, always produced the same way and with the same amount of alcohol and degrees Plato.' The excise duty is based on the degrees Plato or specific gravity of the beer. 'In our brewery that won't be the case.'

For Blonde Stoot, Stout Mokke and the Escort Deluxe beers — Cabardouche's signature beers — they intend to stick to contract brewing, at Brouwerij Anders, knowing that in the craft beer scene it is quite controversial. 'We know contract brewing is looked down upon. A lot of beer companies hire another brewery to brew their beers for them and some aren't transparent about it, but as long as we are I don't see the problem,' Elise declares. 'Our most popular beers are brewed by Anders. But it's still our recipe and they brew it well. By choosing this approach we can limit the amount of investments and keep our hands and minds free to experiment with limited editions.'

MURPHY'S LAW

Twenty days after the shareholders' meeting the brewhouse is finally delivered. It will take two days to put it together. When Elise brings me the news she is really excited, relieved even. They will do a water test, she tells me, before they plan a maiden brew session. Nele and I are eager to follow their story and would like to join them the first time they brew inside their railway arch. I'm curious about the experience of brewing while trains rumble overhead. I experienced the sensation — and the noise — during the shareholders' meeting.

Because all five brewers of Cabardouche still work day jobs — they don't make a living out of brewing yet — there is some time in between brewdays and they have often taken place during weekends and holidays (when the excise duty procedure will have been completed the new archway brewery at the Centers will be open on Fridays, which will also be the fixed brewday). On Sunday, when the water test takes place, I send a text message at night, asking how things have gone — the next Wednesday the first real brew session is planned. Bad news again: the brewhouse is leaking, so the brew session is postponed until further notice.

Then it takes a while before I hear from Cabardouche again. And when I do it's... bad news again. The floor tiles started to give in to the weight of the tanks and kettles once they were filled. The Cabardouche brewers had to dismantle and move the brewing installation, retile the mezzanine, and then move the installation back upstairs. It was Murphy's Law put into practice.

Today this is about to change. Today is the first brew session on Cabardouche's brewing installation. It's still a brew test, with some guidance of Erik, the brewhouse technician who has put together the installation. But they will make real beer, a hoppy amber ale with leftover malts from homebrew sessions. Despite the fact that they still can't sell beers brewed in the new brewery — because they can only get a permit from the excise duty officials after the installation has been approved — they give this beer a proper though temporary and ironic name:
No crying over spilled malt.

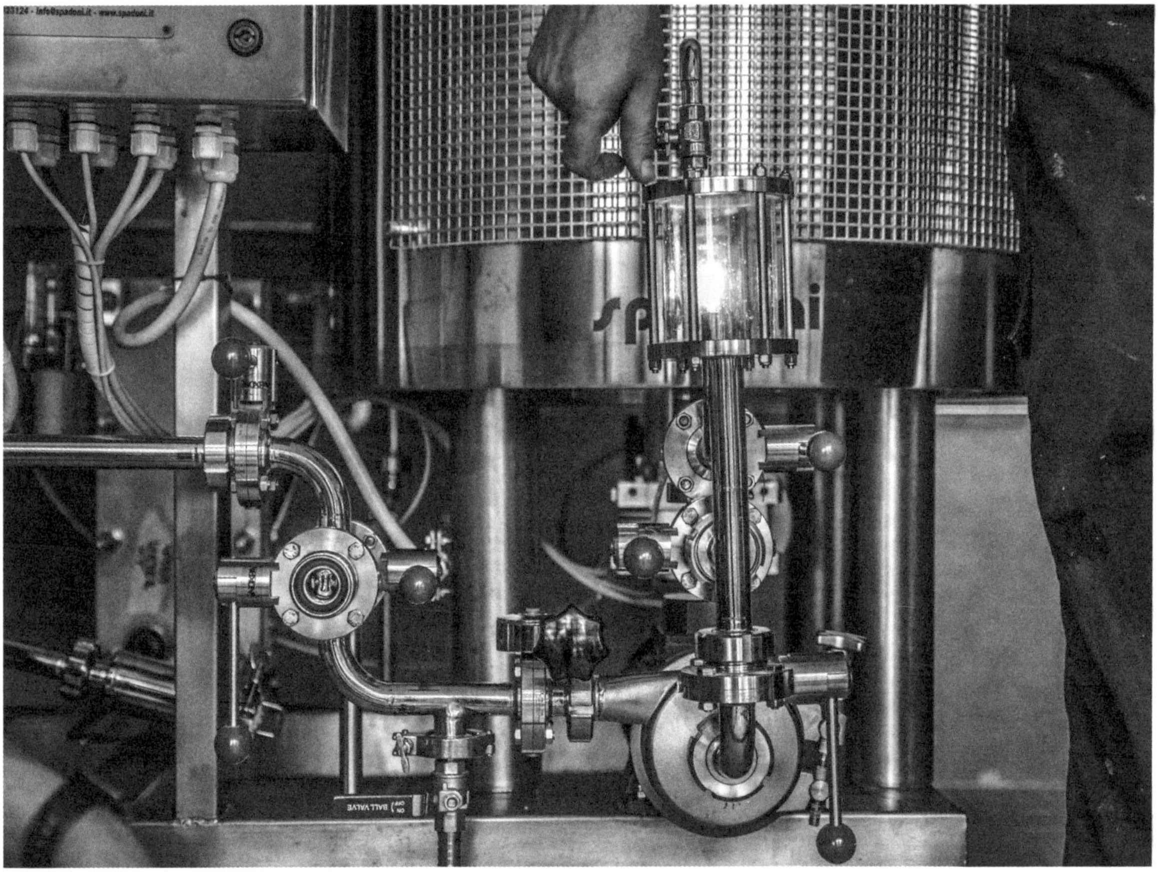

CAUTIOUS RELIEF

'Are you relieved now?' I ask Elise and Stendert, who are doing some paperwork for the brewery while Peter and Igor are monitoring the mashing process with Erik (Jens showed up briefly, but is in the middle of a varnishing job at home). 'We're happy that the first brew session is ongoing, but we're also careful not to be too excited. We'll be relieved when today has passed successfully and the excise duty formalities are over,' Elise says. 'So far we haven't missed any important deadlines, but now two are getting closer. We want to have new beer for Billie's Craft Beer Fest in November, and around the same time a beer should be ready that we've developed for the fifth anniversary of a nearby beer pub. So we would like things to move on now.'

'Peter takes care of the excise duty formalities and he has been told that it should only take a couple of weeks from now,' Stendert adds. Given that he is the man of numbers and figures in Cabardouche (all members brew together, but they have their own responsibilities within the company structure) I ask him whether it was hard to bridge this period of unexpected brewery inactivity. 'Well, we're lucky that our core beers were still brewed at Anders. We had some expenses, like rent, that were not compensated by an income from production here, but we luckily weren't entirely dependent on it,' Stendert explains.

Despite the setbacks the Cabardouche brewers are full of plans. They still stick to the ambition of being a real city brewery like in the old days. They want to work out the idea of beer subscriptions. And they most of all want their brewery to be a fine meeting place for people with good beer ideas who want to come and join the brewers on a brewday.'

Sustainability is vital to their future plans too. Cabardouche is participating in projects developing reground beer crates and recycled kegs and has plans to bring the spent grains to a local children's farm and a mushroom farmer. And they want to grow their own hops in the future.

But above all they want to brew accessible beers and specialty beers for a reasonable price, so that many people will be able to taste them.

210

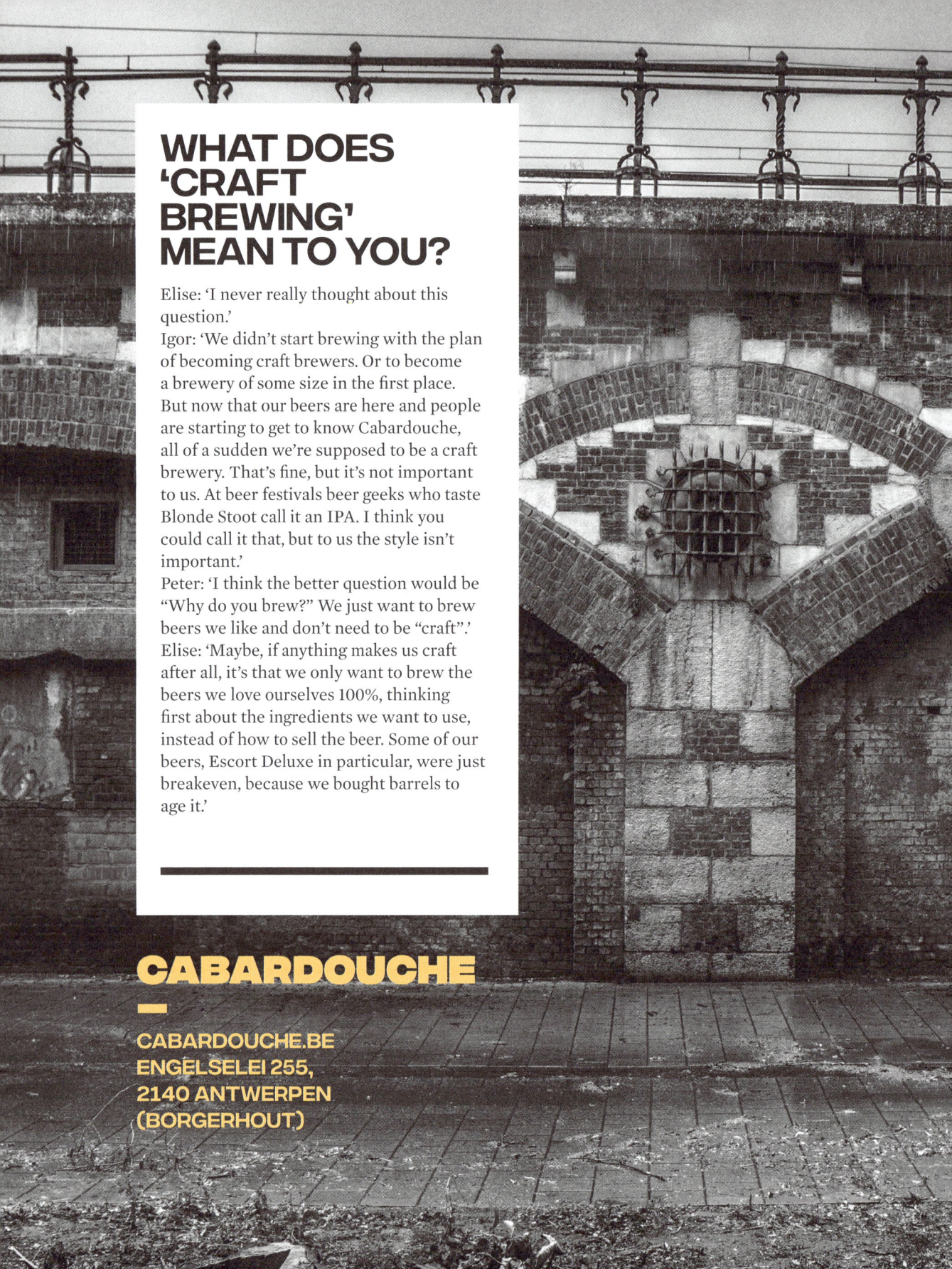

THE SIGNATURE BEERS OF CABARDOUCHE

BLONDE STOOT
(5% ABV)

A thirst-quenching blond that shares some characteristics with saisons and pale ales. Low in alcohol, but with a clear character, this one is a crowd pleaser. It's hoppy and fruity with a subtle citrus aroma and some esters in the nose, and leaves an easy-drinking, well-carbonated impression on the palate, with a malty flavour followed by a pronounced but gentle bitterness.

STOUT MOKKE
(9% ABV)

Called a Belgian stout by the brewers, this sweet imperial stout is a nice one to accompany dessert, with an aroma of coffee and caramel and similar flavours accompanied by some notes of liquorice and chocolate. While sweetness is prominent at first it is nicely balanced by a surfacing bitterness of roasted malts and bittering hops.

ESCORT DELUXE

Cabardouche's Escort Deluxe is released once a year, but every time it's a different beer, an uncommon style or made with surprising ingredients. The last two Escort Deluxe editions also contain a 'luxurious' amount of alcohol. In 2016 it was a salty gose with sea buckthorn of 8% ABV. 2017 had two editions of a barley wine with pear of 13% ABV, of which one was aged in oak barrels of the Belgian Owl whisky. And in 2018 the Escort Deluxe was a caramel stout of 13% ABV. Too much of these escorts and your machinery might be out of service.

A farmhouse of the mind

SAISON

Saisons or farmhouse ales are traditional beers in Belgium. That's why I was quite surprised that saisons were brewed on four out of eight brewdays when I joined the craft brewers in this book. One of the reasons saisons are so popular among a new generation of brewers and beer lovers is because they make for easy-drinking beers, quite bitter and often crisp, fruity and hoppy sometimes, and above all refreshing but with a strong character.

Saisons are defined as beers made on farms from whatever ingredients were available. But that background definition is open for debate. In the 19th century farmers from the Belgian province of Hainaut certainly brewed their own beers, farmhouse ales if you like, most likely for their seasonal workers, but no source tells us they called it a saison. Beers named saisons were available at the time, but quite often in industrial cities like Charleroi and Liège, and the name was mostly used for brown ales. It appears that the term came into use for the farmhouse ales in the early 20th century.

Today it is a yeast-forward beer. The yeast strain that is used for saisons is one with a huge appetite, one that is greedy for sugar, but takes its time to eat it all. That's why most saisons are dry, but need some time to mature. Another defining element of a saison yeast is the spicy, peppery aroma and flavour it produces. In combination with herbal hops that is the blueprint of a contemporary saison. Historically saisons were probably closer to lambics, but we can't taste any bottles to verify this.

Whatever the origins of the name or the style, I like the idea of a beer made on farms with grains that weren't sold and with wild yeast (unconsciously at first) and later homegrown yeast. Now, I'm not a farmer and growing my own yeast hasn't passed the experimental stage (see page 43-44), but I do like the idea of making a beer with what's at hand. Leftover bread, for instance, some malts I've always got in store like pilsner and wheat, and hops in the freezer from a previous brew.

The leftover bread idea

Beer made with leftover or surplus bread is becoming quite popular. It is one of the brewer's possible answers to become more resource responsible. Brewers can try to reduce the amount of energy or water they use — which makes a huge difference — or they can track down the origins of their ingredients, starting with grains and malts. Using leftover bread for now is more of a symbolic gesture, but if you take into account how much bread is thrown away, especially in larger cities, leftover bread beer might make some difference.

It isn't a coincidence that the brewers or organisations who so far have released a leftover bread beer are from capitals like Brussels and London. Brussels Beer Project released Babylone, described as a bread bitter, in 2015 and claims it is the first beer brewed with leftover bread, in a way going back to the Babylonian origins of beer. They inspired the London-based non-profit organisation behind Toast Ale, a growing project in the UK. According to their website they have used one million slices of bread in beer worldwide so far.

Both Babylone and Toast Ale are pale ales in terms of aroma and flavour, but you could say they are saisons at heart. To quote American beer writer William Bostwick in his book The Brewer's Tale: A History of the World According to Beer: 'Farmhouse beer doesn't need a farmhouse after all. It doesn't need a special recipe, or a cultivated provenance. All it needs is the right attitude — a farmhouse of the mind.'

Saison pain perdu or a leftover bread farmhouse ale

In this recipe the bread will be the unpredictable variable in terms of effect on gravity, colour and taste. The kind of leftover bread you use will play an important role, as will the way that you use it: fresh, dried, roasted... But that's the fun of homebrewing: nobody cares about the consistency of your product, and surprises often make for interesting beers you've probably never tasted before. You can use bread up to one third of the malt bill. But we have to admit that, with an 11 litre batch and leftover bread accounting for only 15% of the grist, you won't save the world.

FOR 11 LITRES

MALT: *2.1 kg of pilsner malt, 300 g of leftover bread and 300 g of wheat malt*
YEAST: *Belle Saison or French Saison*
HOP: *15 g of Brewer's Gold, 30 g of Hallertau tradition, 45 g of Hallertau Blanc and 45 g of Mandarina Bavaria*
EXTRA: *Irish moss*

MASH

— Add 16 litres of water to a kettle and attach the brewbag to the handles of the kettle. Warm up the water to 68°C.

60' — Pour in the milled malts. The water will drop in temperature to about 67°C.
Hold at 67°C for 60 minutes. Gently keep on stirring the malts.

55' — Adjust pH to 5.4.

— Pull out the bag, let it drain. You should be able to start the boil with 15 litres of wort with a pre-boil original gravity of 1042.

BOIL

70' — Start to boil the wort. Just before it starts boiling adjust pH to 5.2.

60' — Boil for 60 minutes. Add Brewer's Gold (15 g).

50' — Add Hallertau tradition (5 g).

40' — Add Hallertau tradition (5 g).

30' — Add Hallertau tradition (5 g).

20' — Add Hallertau tradition (5 g).

10' — Add Irish moss (5g) and Hallertau tradition (10 g).

00' — Add Hallertau Blanc (20 g) and Mandarina Bavaria (20 g). Stop the boil.

FERMENTATION

- Cool down the wort to 25°C.
- Measure the specific gravity of the wort. You should reach an original gravity of 1057. Transfer to the fermentation bucket. About 11 litres should go into the bucket. Sprinkle the dry yeast over the wort.
- Let it ferment for a week at 20–22°C.
- Final gravity should be around 1008, approximately 6.4% ABV.

LAGERING AND DRY-HOPPING

- Transfer the beer to the lagering bucket.
- Dry-hop with Hallertau Blanc (25 g) and Mandarina Bavaria (25 g), and let it lager for another week in a cooler place.

BOTTLING AND BOTTLE CONDITIONING

- Boil 70 g of sugar (7 g per litre, we want fairly high carbonation) in a small amount of water. Let it cool down to 25°C.
- Remove the bags with hops from the bucket and add the sugar water. Gently stir it with a sanitised spoon. Close the lid. You're ready to start bottling.
- Put the bottles in a warm dark place for a week in order to carbonate the beer. Then let them rest for a couple of weeks in a cooler place or a fridge.

BREWING NOTE

- Most saisons are not dry-hopped but have a clear hop profile. In this version I used two craft beer techniques to enhance the hop character: continual hopping (adding smaller doses of hops throughout the boil) and dry-hopping (because I couldn't resist) with some European aroma hops from the freezer: Hallertau Blanc and Mandarina Bavaria. Of course, the degree of hoppiness you want a saison to have is a matter of taste. For a different hop aroma and flavour profile you can add 15 g of Hallertau Blanc and/or Mandarina Bavaria in the last minutes of the boil or when you stop the boil instead of dry-hopping.

33 + 33

craft breweries you need to know

The rising number of Belgian craft beers and craft breweries is part of a global story. Belgian beers are liked and respected all over the world, but the craft beer revolution we see at work worldwide was born in the US. In the course of the last three decades the rest of the world has followed, and so has Belgium.

On this page and the next you will find two lists with craft breweries you should discover: 33 Belgian breweries (on top of the eight I joined for a brewday) and 33 international breweries. For Belgian beer lovers some of the names in the first list will sound familiar, Dutch beer lovers will certainly recognize some Dutch breweries in the second list, etc. With these lists, however, my first intention was to bring a few rather unknown and (relatively) young breweries to a larger audience.

To limit the arbitrary character of such a list — inevitable if you want to select 2 x 33 breweries to discover — I've used the same criteria I used to select the brewers I visited: a transparent way of brewing, focus on the product, authenticity, an open mind and the drive to innovate and collaborate. And above all: all the breweries in the two lists can be linked to one another in one way or another and they form an informal, organic and diverse network. Because they did a collab together, shared a boot at a beer festival, discovered each other in the course of a beer odyssee, or because they follow each other's work closely and I was tipped off by a fellow brewer.

If you use these names and websites to search the internet, you'll get a good idea of what moves in the craft beer world, but of course the lists are no more than a sampler and incomplete. For this book I limited myself to bite-size lists, an easy-drinking 33cl can if you like. Suggestions of breweries I should discover — and I'm sure there are many — can be made on www.beerodysseyinrubberboots.com.

33X BELGIUM

1. **ALVINNE**
   MOEN
   WWW.ALVINNE.COM

2. **BASTARD BREWERS**
   MONS
   BASTARDBREWERS.BEER

3. **BOKKE**
   HASSELT
   WWW.BOKKE.BE

4. **BRASSERIE À VAPEUR**
   PIPAIX
   WWW.VAPEUR.COM

5. **BRASSERIE DE LA SAMBRE**
   SPY
   BRASSERIEDELASAMBRE.COM

6. **BRASSERIE DE LA SENNE**
   SINT-JANS-MOLENBEEK
   WWW.BRASSERIEDELASENNE.BE

7. **BRASSERIE DU BRABANT**
   BAISY-THY

8. **BRASSERIE MINNE**
BAILLONVILLE
BRASSERIEMINNE.BE

9. **BRASSERIE SAINTE-HÉLÈNE**
FLORENVILLE
SAINTE-HELENE.BE

10. **BROUWBAR**
GHENT

11. **BROUWERIJ BROERS**
WACHTEBEKE
WWW.BROUWERIJBROERS.BE

12. **BROUWERIJ D'OUDE MAALDERIJ**
IZEGEM
WWW.DOUDEMAALDERIJ.COM

13. **BROUWERIJ MAENHOUT**
PITTEM
WWW.BROUWERIJMAENHOUT.BE

14. **BROUWERIJ RUIMTEGIST**
KORTRIJK
RUIMTEGIST.BE

15. **BRUSSELS BEER PROJECT**
BRUSSELS
WWW.BEERPROJECT.BE

16. **DE DOCHTER VAN DE KORENAAR**
BAARLE-HERTOG
WWW.DEDOCHTERVANDEKORENAAR.BE

17. **DE LAATSTE DRINKER**
GHENT
WWW.DELAATSTEDRINKER.BE

18. **DE PLUKKER**
POPERINGE
WWW.PLUKKER.BE

19. **EN STOEMELINGS**
BRUSSELS
ENSTOEMELINGS.BE

20. **FANTÔME**
SOY
WWW.FANTOME.BE

21. **GALEA CRAFT BEERS**
BRASSCHAAT
WWW.GALEACRAFTBEERS.BE

22. **GISTGEEST**
ANTWERP
WWW.GISTGEEST.BE

23. **GUEUZERIE TILQUIN**
BIERGHES
WWW.GUEUZERIETILQUIN.BE

24. **HOF TEN DORMAAL**
TILDONK
HOFTENDORMAAL.COM

25. **HUMBOLDT & GAUSS**
GHENT
WWW.HUMBOLDTENGAUSS.BE

26. **LA SOURCE**
BRUSSELS
WWW.LASOURCEBEER.BE

27. **NO SCIENCE BRASSERIE**
BRUSSELS
NOSCIENCE.BE

28. **NOVABIRRA**
BRAINE-L'ALLEUD
WWW.NOVABIRRA.COM

29. **STADSBROUWERIJ 'T KOELSCHIP**
OOSTEND

30. **TALL POPPY BREWING**
KONTICH
WWW.TALLPOPPY.BE

31. **THE NOMAD BEER PROJECT**
LIÈGE/ANTWERP
NOMADBEERPROJECT.BE

32. **TOTEM**
EVERGEM
TOTEMBEER.COM

33. **VLEESMEESTER BREWERY**
EDEGEM
VLEESMEESTERBREWERY.BE

33X INTERNATIONAL

Brazil

1. **CERVEJARIA DÁDIVA**
   VÁRZEA PAULISTA, SÃO PAULO

Canada

2. **BIG AXE BREWERY**
   NACKAWIC, NEW BRUNSWICK
   BIGAXE.CA

3. **LE TROU DU DIABLE**
   SHAWINIGAN, QUÉBEC
   TROUDUDIABLE.COM

China

4. **BUBBLE LAB BREWING**
   WUHAN

Denmark

5. **TO ØL**
   COPENHAGEN
   TOOLBEER.DK

Estonia

6. **TANKER**
   HARJU MAAKOND
   TANKER.EE

France

7. **SINGE SAVANT**
   LILLE
   SINGE-SAVANT.COM

Germany

8. **SCHNEEEULE**
BERLIN
WP.SCHNEEEULE.BERLIN

Great Britain

9. **40FT**
LONDON
WWW.40FTBREWERY.COM

10. **NORTHERN MONK**
LEEDS
NORTHERNMONK.COM

11. **YONDER**
BINEGAR
WWW.BREWYONDER.CO.UK

Hungary

12. **MONYO BREWING CO.**
BUDAPEST
MONYOBREWING.COM

Ireland

13. **GALWAY BAY BREWERY**
GALWAY
GALWAYBAYBREWERY.COM

Israel

14. **DANCING CAMEL BREWERY**
TEL AVIV
DANCINGCAMEL.COM

Italy

15. **MAESTRI DEL SANNIO**
CERRETO SANNITA
WWW.MAESTRIDELSANNIO.IT

16. **MUKKELER**
PORTO SANT'ELPIDIO
MUKKELLER.IT

17. **STRADAREGINA**
VIGEVANO
BIRRIFICIOSTRADAREGINA.WEEBLY.COM

Luxembourg

18. **TOTENHOPFEN BRAUHAUS**
LUXEMBOURG
WWW.TOTENHOPFEN-BRAUHAUS.COM

Netherlands

19. **DE MOERSLEUTEL**
ALKMAAR
BROUWERIJDEMOERSLEUTEL.NL

20. **NEVEL**
NIJMEGEN
NEVEL.ORG

21. **VAN MOLL**
EINDHOVEN
VANMOLLCRAFTBEER.COM

Norway

22. **LERVIG AKTIEBRYGGERI**
STAVANGER
WWW.LERVIG.NO

Portugal

23. **8A COLINA**
LISBON
WWW.OITAVACOLINA.PT

Slovenia

24. **RESERVOIR DOGS**
NOVA GORICA
RESERVOIR-DOGS.BEER

Spain

25. BIDASSOA BASQUE BREWERY
IRUN
WWW.BIDASSOA.ES

26. LA CALAVERA
GIRONA
WWW.LACALAVERA.CAT

27. LA QUINCE
MADRID
LAQUINCEBREWERY.COM

Sweden

28. TEMPEL BRYGGHUS
UPPSALA
TEMPELBRYGGHUS.SE

Switserland

29. À TUE-TÊTE
AIGLE

Ukraine

30. VARVAR BREW
KIEV
VARVARBREW.COM

United States of America

31. HALFWAY CROOKS BREWING AND BLENDING
ATLANTA

32. PEN DRUID BREWING
SPARRYVILLE, VIRGINIA
PENDRUID.COM

33. WICKED WEED BREWING
ASHEVILLE, NOORD-CAROLINA
WWW.WICKEDWEEDBREWING.COM

RECOMMENDED READING

BAETSLÉ, GILBERT
—*De praktijkbrouwer* —
Academia Press, 2015

BOSTWICK, WILLIAM
—*The Brewer's Tale. A History of the World According to Beer* —
W. W. Norton & Company, 2014

HEALY, JULIAN
—*The Hops List. 265 Beer Hop Varieties From Around the World* —
Blurb, 2018

HINDY, STEVE
—*The Craft Beer Revolution. How a Band of Microbrewers Is Transforming the World's Favorite Drink* —
Palgrave Macmillan Ltd, 2015

PAUWELS, LUC
—*Bier brouwen voor starters* —
Standaard Uitgeverij, 2012

ROBERTS, DINAH
—*The Lazy All-Grain Brewster: Keeping It Simple* —
Eigen beheer, 2018

ROGERS, CHRISTOPHER
—*Brew In a Bag: Brew fantastic craft beers at home using the All Grain brew in a bag method* —
Brewinabag UK, 2016

TIERNEY-JONES, ADRIAN
—*1001 Beers You Must Try before You Die* —
Cassell Illustrated, 2011

TONSMEIRE, MICHAEL
—*American Sour Beers. Innovative Techniques for Mixed Fermentations* —
Brewers Publications, 2014

WEBSITES

beerandbrewing.com
byo.com
homebrewersassociation.org
www.brewcabin.com
www.brewersfriend.com
www.themadfermentationist.com

ACKNOWLEDGMENTS

Writing a book is an intensive enterprise that travels many, often winding roads. Ideas come, and go. And they come from all directions, not just from the inspiration of the author. He is the one who is met with applause — let's hope there will be applause — but the hard work to make this book possible has been done by many hands.

I would like to thank Nele Pierlet for the lovely pictures and for accompanying me on this beer odyssee, director-publisher Johan Ghysels for believing in this project, and editor Thomas Van der Goten for coordinating it, and for the interesting talks and the necessary feedback that helped to turn an idea into a finished book. I would also like to thank graphic designer Tom Suykens and the copy editors Tamsin Shelton and Jan Vangansbeke for their contribution to image and word, and brewer Janos De Baets and beer connoisseur Daniella Provost for checking facts, figures, background information and beer recipes.

Writing a book also requires making choices and comes with ups and downs and alternating moments of enthusiasm, despair, relief, sighing and cursing, hyperactivity, decompression and — let's not forget — a lot of pleasure. But more than the author it is the loved ones, with a front-row seat, who sometimes get to suffer, being the first to buffer when the tension rises. That's why, above all, I would like to thank my two sons Korneel and Pepijn and my wife Carmen Vandeputte for their support, their patience and the many fresh, unbiased ideas they came up with. Exactly what a father and husband needs when his thoughts are wandering to some remote place, where text, brewkettles, beer and rubber boots rule. They helped me to focus again on what really matters.

COLOPHON

WWW.LANNOO.COM
Register on our web site and we will regularly send you a newsletter with information about new books and interesting, exclusive offers.

TEXT
Jeroen Bert
PHOTOGRAPHY
Nele Pierlet
GRAPHIC DESIGN
Tom Suykens

If you have observations or questions, please contact our editorial office: redactielifestyle@lannoo.com

© Lannoo Publishers, Tielt, 2019
D/2019/45/554 — NUR 448
ISBN 978 94 014 6478 9

All rights reserved. Nothing from this publication may be copied, stored in an automated database and/or be made public in any form or in any way, either electronic, mechanical or in any other manner without the prior written consent of the publisher.